Whitehead's Metaphysics of Power

To Pietro, active substance

The riddle of the universe is not so easy.
A. N. Whitehead

Whitehead's Metaphysics of Power
Reconstructing Modern Philosophy

Pierfrancesco Basile

Edinburgh University Press is one of the leading university presses in the UK.
We publish academic books and journals in our selected subject areas across the
humanities and social sciences, combining cutting-edge scholarship with high
editorial and production values to produce academic works of lasting importance.
For more information visit our website: edinburghuniversitypress.com

© Pierfrancesco Basile, 2017

Edinburgh University Press Ltd
The Tun – Holyrood Road, 12(2f) Jackson's Entry, Edinburgh EH8 8PJ

Typeset in 11/14 Adobe Sabon by
IDSUK (DataConnection) Ltd

A CIP record for this book is available from the British Library

ISBN 978 1 4744 0414 3 (hardback)
ISBN 978 1 4744 0415 0 (webready PDF)
ISBN 978 1 4744 0416 7 (epub)

The right of Pierfrancesco Basile to be identified as the author of this work has been
asserted in accordance with the Copyright, Designs and Patents Act 1988, and the
Copyright and Related Rights Regulations 2003 (SI No. 2498).

Contents

Preface vii
Acknowledgements xi
Abbreviations xiii

Part I In Search of a New Metaphysics
1 Introduction: Metaphysics, Science, Common Sense 3
2 Speculative Metaphysics: Defining the Ideal 17

Part II From Permanence to Process
3 Deconstructing Tradition: Substance Revisited 31
4 The Flowing Self: From Monads to Actual Occasions 47
5 Overcoming the Cartesian Legacy: The Process Concept of Substance 61

Part III From Process to Permanence
6 Changing Shapes of Reality: Understanding Nature under a Social Analogy 79
7 Theological Afterthoughts: A Neo-Platonic God for a Darwinian Universe? 101

8 Conclusion: The Ethics of Creativity – A Deweyan Critique 115

*Appendix: The Making of a Metaphysician –
A Biographical Note* 129
Bibliography 133
Index 141

Preface

Among the truly outstanding philosophers of the twentieth century, Alfred North Whitehead holds the unenviable status of being the most neglected. Before the outbreak of the Second World War he was widely acclaimed as one of the great thinkers of the times. After that tragic event, the philosophical world in both Britain and the USA changed radically. Academics now perceived themselves as professionals with their own field of expertise;[1] Whitehead's metaphysical writings, which are full of daring speculations into the ultimate nature of things, could hardly exert any great attraction on philosophers hypnotised by the fabulous *minutiae* of logic and linguistic analysis.

Because of the oblivion into which it fell in the second half of the last century, Whitehead's process metaphysics remains comparatively little known.[2] It is ignored, rather than rejected on philosophical grounds. This is regrettable, for Whitehead dealt in unconventional

---

[1] These developments have been recently analysed by Stuart Brown in 'The Professionalization of British Philosophy', in W. Mander (ed.), *The Oxford Handbook of British Philosophy in the Nineteenth Century*, Oxford: Oxford University Press, 2014, pp. 619–40. See also G. Ryle, 'Fifty Years of Philosophy and Philosophers', *Philosophy* 51, 1976, pp. 381–9, and J. O. Urmson, *Philosophical Analysis. Its Development between the Two World Wars*, Oxford: Clarendon Press, 1956, esp. pp. 163–200.

[2] Whitehead's influence has been stronger in the USA, where a vigorous (yet unfortunately somewhat militant) school of process philosophy and theology has arisen around the remarkable figures of Charles Hartshorne, John Cobb and David Ray Griffin. There has been a forceful revival of interest in recent years in continental Europe, especially in countries with strong metaphysical traditions such as Germany and France. Reception of Whitehead's ideas, and especially of his later metaphysics, has been much more limited in the UK, where only a few (though excellent) scholars such as Dorothy Emmett, Ivor Leclerc, Wolfe Mays, Timothy Sprigge and Peter Simons have devoted serious critical attention to his thought.

fashion with questions that are at the centre of contemporary debates, especially in ontology and the philosophy of mind. Some prominent analytic philosophers working in these fields are even travelling intellectual paths closely resembling Whitehead's own, apparently without fully realising it.

This book aims at making Whitehead's complex system accessible to a wider audience than it currently enjoys. It is by no means to be regarded as a complete interpretation of his worldview. Nevertheless, an effort has been made to elucidate all the basic principles that ground his vision and, most importantly perhaps, the problems to which his philosophy is supposed to provide an answer. At the same time, and following Whitehead's own practice, I have tried to show how he reached his sometimes very counter-intuitive conclusions by way of dialogue with the great masters of the past – Plato and Aristotle, but also early modern philosophers like Descartes, Newton, Locke, Hume and Spinoza. A prominent place in the following reconstruction is occupied by Leibniz, who is, together with Plato, Whitehead's true philosophical hero.

There are deep philosophical motivations behind Whitehead's engagement with such great figures. As he explains in his *magnum opus*, *Process and Reality* (1929), our thinking is held captive by old ideas unconsciously held. What philosophy stands in need of is a conceptual revolution – a critique of tradition that would also enable us to develop a radically new way of conceiving of the world and our place in it.

The following exposition is divided into three main parts. Part I, 'In Search of a New Metaphysics', examines why Whitehead deemed it necessary to engage in metaphysics in the first place and how he thought speculation had to be practised in order to remain a respectable intellectual enterprise. Part II, 'From Permanence to Process', focuses on the concept of the 'actual occasion', the event-like, powerfully active unit that in his theory plays the role performed by the concept of substance in traditional metaphysical systems. Actual occasions are the most basic realities, the fundamental elements upon which all other things depend for their existence. Finally Part III, 'From Process to Permanence', shows how Whitehead constructed (or better perhaps, began to construct) a system of reality upon the basis provided by his new understanding of substance. How can there be permanence and order in a world whose ultimate constituents are fleeting events? This is a main problem for any process metaphysics and Whitehead's solution will be explained in this concluding part.

This little book has been written with the general philosophical reader in mind. Its most immediate aim is to present Whitehead as an author still eminently worth reading – or, more courageously put, as one who deserves to be rediscovered. I have not refrained from criticising his position, however, and I hope that the following pages may also be of interest to the specialised scholar.

Acknowledgements

Portions of three previously published articles – 'Overcoming the Legacy of Modern Thought: Whitehead's Revisionary Metaphysics of Mind and Nature', *Routledge Handbook of Panpsychism*, forthcoming 2017; 'Learning from Leibniz: Whitehead (and Russell) on Mind, Matter and Monads', *British Journal for the History of Philosophy* 23/6, 2015, pp. 1128–49; and 'Philosophy, Creativity and the Good: Dewey's Critique of Whitehead's Metaphysics', *Process Studies* 42/1, 2013, pp. 5–19 – have been incorporated, and adapted to the purposes of the present book, in Chapters 2, 4 and 8. Over the years, I have learned much from conversations with many scholars and philosophers. I cannot name all of them here. A special word of thanks, however, is due to Peter Simons for brief but penetrating discussions, and Galen Strawson for precious comments on a previous version of this essay.

Abbreviations

AG	G. W. Leibniz, *Philosophical Essays*, ed. and trans. R. Ariew and D. Garber, Indianapolis: Hackett, 1989
AI	A. N. Whitehead, *Adventures of Ideas* [1933], New York: The Free Press, 1967
CN	A. N. Whitehead, *The Concept of Nature* [1920], Cambridge: Cambridge University Press, 2000
EN	J. Dewey, *Experience and Nature* [1925], New York: Dover, 1958
ERE	W. James, *Essays in Radical Empiricism*, New York: Longmans, Green, 1912
ESP	A. N. Whitehead, *Essays in Science and Philosophy*, London: Rider, 1948
MT	A. N. Whitehead, *Modes of Thought* [1938], New York: The Free Press, 1969
PL	B. Russell, *A Critical Exposition of the Philosophy of Leibniz* [1900], London: George Allen and Unwin, 1937
PM	B. Russell, *Portraits from Memory and Other Essays*, London: George Allen and Unwin, 1956
PP	W. James, *The Principles of Psychology*, vol. I, New York: Dover, 1890
PR	A. N. Whitehead, *Process and Reality: An Essay in Cosmology* [1929], corrected edition by D. R. Griffin and D. W. Sherburne, New York: The Free Press, 1978
PW	J. Dewey, 'The Philosophy of Whitehead', in P. A. Schilpp (ed.), *The Philosophy of Alfred North Whitehead*, La Salle, IL: Open Court, 1941, pp. 641–61

RIP   J. Dewey, *Reconstruction in Philosophy* [1920], Boston: Beacon Press, 1948
RM   A. N. Whitehead, *Religion in the Making*, Cambridge: Cambridge University Press, 1926
SMW   A. N. Whitehead, *Science and the Modern World* [1925], New York: The Free Press, 1967

PART I

In Search of a New Metaphysics

CHAPTER I

Introduction: Metaphysics, Science, Common Sense

PROCESS METAPHYSICS AND THE LANGUAGE PROBLEM

In terms of current philosophical classifications, Whitehead is an exponent of 'process philosophy'. Philosophical denominations are difficult to pin down to a precise definition, but in this case there is a clear-cut criterion for distinguishing between process and non-process thinkers. Common sense takes it for granted that all activities and happenings are to be traced back to some pre-existing entity. It was Peter, we say, who let our aunt's precious cup fall on the ground; and the falling is not a ghostly floating occurrence: it is the falling *of* the aunt's cup. In our ordinary conceptual scheme, permanent things have priority over events. They are, to use P. F. Strawson's apt terminology, the 'basic particulars'.[1]

Whitehead does not question that the common-sense view is pragmatically useful, but he takes a revisionary approach when questions of basic ontology are at stake. At a metaphysically fundamental level, he posits *processes* rather than *things* as the building blocks of reality. The idea that the category of process is ontologically fundamental is not easy to understand. What kinds of processes are basic? How is their nature to be discovered? How are permanence and stability to be accounted for in a world whose ultimate constituents are ongoing process-units? What kind of worldview can be constructed around this central intuition? How are we to evaluate its validity?

Before considering Whitehead's answers to these questions in the following chapters, a word is in order concerning one major difficulty that any process philosophy has to face. Process metaphysics effects a radical alteration of our ordinary conceptions. Such modes of thought are very old, however, and have left an indelible mark upon our language. A truly revisionary metaphysics must therefore not solely provide a new conceptual scheme, but also a new language in which to articulate it. As Whitehead puts it:

> Every science must devise its own instruments. The tool
> required for philosophy is language. Thus philosophy redesigns
> language in the same way that, in a physical science,
> pre-existing appliances are redesigned. (PR 11)

The seriousness of the problem becomes evident as soon as one realises that the ontology of enduring things is mirrored in the subject–predicate structure of natural language. In order to correctly express a radically different conceptual scheme, one would therefore have to revise not solely the available vocabulary, but *grammar* as well. In philosophy, Whitehead says, 'linguistic discussion is a tool, but should never be a master. Language is imperfect both in its words and in its *forms*' (AI 228; my emphasis). This sounds like a difficult, perhaps impossible task. It is as if the revisionary metaphysician has either to attempt an extraordinary transmutation of ordinary language, or try to communicate his worldview from within a medium that incorporates opposite theoretical commitments. In fact, Whitehead will mostly steer a middle course, *twisting* ordinary language and traditional philosophical terminology in the hope of eliciting new meanings.

Contrary to a widespread philosophical prejudice, Whitehead denies in *Adventures of Ideas* that the limits of language are the limits of thought:

> Language delivers its evidence in three chapters, one on
> the meanings of words, another on the meanings enshrined
> in grammatical forms, and the third, on meanings beyond
> individual words and beyond grammatical forms, meanings
> miraculously revealed in great literature. (AI 226)

Not only philosophy, but also science is constantly confronted with the task of revising the language we have inherited from our ancestors. In this respect, Whitehead suggests, philosophy and science do not differ from literature and poetry; they are all engaged in the common task of 'finding linguistic expressions for meanings as yet unexpressed' (AI 227).

In spite of Whitehead's confidence in the transcendent powers of human thought, it would be idle to deny that the problem posed by language constitutes a strong *prima facie* objection against revisionary metaphysics. But it is less than a proof of its impossibility. For the time being, the point to be appreciated is that the strangeness of Whitehead's terminology is not a result of philosophical incapacity, but the proper response to a real problem. To appeal to this feature of his writings as an argument against his philosophy would demonstrate failure in understanding the enterprise he is engaged in, not superior philosophical *acumen*.

WHAT SCIENTIFIC MATERIALISM CANNOT DO

Another startling aspect of Whitehead's metaphysics is his forceful rejection of the notion of insentient material particles, a conception he refers to in *Process and Reality* as the 'doctrine of vacuous actualities' (PR xiii). In *Science and the Modern World*, the new metaphysics of process is offered as an alternative to

> the fixed scientific cosmology which presupposes the ultimate fact of an irreducible brute matter, or material, spread throughout space in a flux of configurations. In itself such material is senseless, valueless, purposeless. It just does what it does do, following a fixed routine imposed by external relations which do not spring from the nature of its being. (SMW 17)

In Whitehead's interpretation, modern science adopted as its ontological framework a materialistic atomism uncritically derived from antiquity. For the limited purposes of ordering and predicting a restricted class of phenomena, this ontology worked perfectly. But fundamental questions remained unanswered. On a materialistic basis, for example, it is impossible to understand why there should be living, experiencing organisms. There is nothing in the idea of inert bits of matter that enables us to *see* why they should give rise to life and experience. The mutual relationships of material particles may be conceived as becoming increasingly complicated in the course of evolution. Nevertheless, the problem of understanding the transition from the purely material aggregate to the living sentient organism remains. As Whitehead has it: '[A] thoroughgoing evolutionary philosophy is inconsistent with materialism. The aboriginal stuff, or material, from which a materialistic philosophy starts is incapable of evolution' (SMW 107).

Whitehead is here giving a new emphasis to an old idea. The reason why *mind* cannot be explained in terms of *matter* is that they have absolutely nothing in common. It is the absolute *heterogeneity* of their natures that prevents understanding of how the former could be derived from the latter. This is the same intuition that generates the problem of accounting for mind–body interaction in the philosophy of Descartes and that eventually led Spinoza to the conclusion that they do not interact after all, 'mind' (the attribute of *thought*) and 'body' (the attribute of *extension*) being only two manifestations of a single Substance.[2]

Whitehead's anti-materialist reasoning also bears a strong similarity to Leibniz's Mill-Argument in the *Monadology*. Contemplate the material machine as much as you will, enlarge it and step into it in your imagination. Still, you will not find anything there that *explains* why the material machine should *also* be thinking. In a letter to Lady Masham, commenting upon Locke's suggestion that God may endow matter with a power to think, Leibniz makes the point even more forcefully:

> It is true that the illustrious Locke maintained in his excellent *Essay* . . . that God can give matter the power of thinking, because he can make everything we can conceive happen. But then matter would think only by a perpetual miracle, since there is nothing in matter in itself, that is, in extension and impenetrability, *from which thought could be deduced*, or upon which it could be based. (AG 290; my emphasis)

God could give matter the power of thinking; *matter* could never generate thought. Why? If there is nothing to matter but extension and impenetrability, the origination of mind out of matter would be a brute fact. If matter and mind happen to be conjoined, this connection would have to be established by an external agency (God) as well as *explicable* by reference to it:

God, in the case of thinking matter, must not only *give* matter the capacity to think, but he must also *maintain* it continually by the same miracle, *since this capacity has no root*, unless God gives matter a new nature. (AG 290; my emphasis)

One can see Leibniz and Whitehead as addressing what is nowadays called the 'hard' problem of consciousness. This is, in brief, how their critique of materialism works:

1. There must be an explanation of everything that is – of its very existence as well as of its specific way of being. (This is an implicit assumption, corresponding to the Principle of Sufficient Reason, according to which all happenings are, in principle, intelligible.)
2. Mental events (such things as thoughts, memories, sensations, emotions) undoubtedly exist.
3. There is nothing in the concept of a material (merely extended) atom or in that of their combination into larger material aggregates that helps explain why mental events shall exist.
4. Hence, materialism – the view that only material atoms truly are and anything else must be explained by reference to them – cannot be the last word about the nature of reality.

Of course, such an argument is not immune from attacks. Eliminative materialists may want to reject (2), for example, while believers in radical emergence would deny (3). But how convincing would their alleged refutations be? It seems preposterous to pretend, as eliminative philosophers do, that mental states are not genuine realities but theoretical posits introduced to account for our physical, publicly observable behaviour. At the same time, it is really impossible to understand how material particles could generate thoughts, if mind and matter are conceived under seventeenth-century Cartesian conceptions. These old categories surely stand in need of a drastic revision. Nor can (1), the Principle of Sufficient Reason, be easily renounced. It is true that we do not know with certainty that all happenings have an explanation. Nevertheless, that things can be explained is something the speculative mind is forced to *postulate* if it does not want to limit itself to the registration of observed regularities.[3] Whitehead gets it exactly right when he says that speculation 'obtains its urge from *a deep ultimate faith*, that through and through the nature of things is penetrable by reason' (AI 108; my emphasis). As a matter of fact, what may be called the Leibniz–Whitehead argument against materialism is a very strong one – as good as any of the best proofs in philosophy.

THE HETEROGENEITY PROBLEM: A SURPRISING IMPLICATION

What does the argument just considered tell us about the intrinsic nature of reality? The intuitive notion that heterogeneous natures cannot interact has highly counterintuitive implications when placed within an evolutionary context. Since human minds undoubtedly exist and have originated in the course of evolution, they must be derived from constituents that are (at least in part) themselves mental. The similar must be derived from the similar, for otherwise there would be a miraculous break in evolutionary continuity. As William James put it in a book Whitehead admired, *The Principles of Psychology* (1890), the appearance of mentality in the course of evolution must be more than an unfathomable *creatio ex nihilo*:

> The point which as evolutionists we are bound to hold fast to is that all the new forms of being that make their appearance are really nothing more than results of the redistribution of the original and unchanging materials. The self-same atoms which, chaotically dispersed, made the nebula, now, jammed and temporarily caught in peculiar positions, form our brains; and the 'evolution' of the brains, if understood, would simply be the account of how the atoms came to be so caught and jammed. In this story no new *natures*, no factors not present at the beginning, are introduced at any later stage.
>   But with the dawn of consciousness an entirely new nature seems to slip in, something whereof the potency was *not* given in the mere outward atoms of the original chaos. (PP 146)

This argument may be briefly stated thus:

1. Because of their radical heterogeneity, mind cannot be derived from matter.
2. Human minds originated in the course of evolution.

3. Hence, they must have originated from constituents that are themselves mental in nature.

This reasoning immediately leads to the *panpsychistic* conclusion that human experience is a basic feature of all things – that is to say, the view that the ultimate constituents of reality are not 'vacuous', but endowed with an inner life of their own.[4] In terms that should strike one as strangely familiar, Whitehead praises Leibniz for having explained 'what it must be like to be an atom' (AI 132).

Isn't this a ludicrous view, one that should be rejected without further ado by any thinking person?[5] Charges of intrinsic implausibility are always difficult to adjudicate in philosophy. The danger is that we condemn as absurd all views inconsistent with our longstanding prejudices. In *Science and the Modern World* Whitehead tries to mitigate any initial resistance we may have by reminding us that the notion of senseless matter is a conceptual construction, a *cultural product*[6] that, as such, can be subjected to criticism, revised or even totally abandoned. Shortly before the rise of Cartesianism, Whitehead observes, even a methodologically cautious author like Francis Bacon found it appropriate to write in his *Sylva Sylvarum: A Natural History* (1627) a sentence such as the following: 'It is certain that all bodies whatsoever, though they have no sense, yet they have perception' (SMW 41).

As Whitehead sees things, the materialist conception of reality so much permeates our mind that it now blocks our view, fatally hindering our speculative imagination:

> We are now so used to the materialistic way of looking at things, which has been rooted in our literature by the genius of the seventeenth century, that it is with some difficulty that we understand the possibility of another mode of approach to the problems of nature. (SMW 42)

Or, as he declares in one of his most thought-provoking passages:

> Men can be provincial in time, as well as in place. We may ask ourselves whether the scientific mentality of the modern world in the immediate past is not a successful example of such provincial limitation. (SMW vii)

A panpsychist view of nature, Whitehead also explains, would not be unscientific. There is a division of labour between physical science and metaphysics: '[S]cience ignores what anything is in itself. Its entities are merely considered in respect to their extrinsic reality, that is to say, in respect to their aspects in other things' (SMW 153). Since science and philosophy ask different questions, there can be no incompatibility between them. A panpsychist view of the ultimate constituents of reality is not solely coherent with science; it may even be what is needed in order to give some content to its rather empty abstractions: 'a complete existence is not a composition of mathematical formulae, mere formulae. It is a concrete composition of things illustrating formulae' (AI 158).[7]

In general, Whitehead holds, one must be guarded against committing the 'fallacy of misplaced concreteness'. This is the mistake, to which the philosopher is prone to fall victim as much as the scientist, of confounding abstract descriptions and described realities. The happenings in nature, Whitehead reminds us, are always more than the theories we have ingeniously devised to handle them.

AGAINST MATERIALISM: TWO ALTERNATIVES

All this is correct as far as it goes. But the rejection of materialism is consistent with two different views of reality's ultimate principles. These are the competing alternatives:

1. on one conception, such principles are *psycho-physical* units, possessing a mental as well as a physical side;
2. on another (idealist or mentalist) conception, such principles are purely *mental*.

Among the early modern thinkers, Leibniz provides a good example of a philosopher who takes both options seriously. The main difficulty for anyone holding (2) is to account for the status of the physical world. Reasoning as a full-fledged metaphysical idealist, Leibniz sometimes suggests that material bodies could only be the phenomenal appearances of groups of monads imperfectly perceived. Interpreted as thus having a firm ground in reality (*phenomena bene fundata*), the material things of everyday experience would occupy a position halfway between full reality and illusory appearance.

On the last page of his copy of George Berkeley's *A Treatise Concerning the Principles of Human Knowledge* (1710), for example, Leibniz objects to the Irish philosopher's account of physical bodies as bundles of perceived ideas as follows:

> There is much here that is correct and close to my own view. But it is expressed paradoxically. For it is not necessary to say that matter is nothing, but it is sufficient to say that it is a phenomenon, like the rainbow; and that it is not a substance, but the resultant of substances. (AG 307)

Leibniz compares the status of material objects with that of the rainbow – which we cannot touch (hence is somewhat less than fully real) but which can nevertheless be perceived by more than one person (hence is more than a private illusion). Eventually, and although this is highly controversial, Leibniz may be seen as a philosopher who is not clear as to which option to choose.[8]

In *Science and the Modern World*, Whitehead clearly favours the psycho-physical conception. Nowhere does he attempt to reduce the physical world to a phenomenal appearance in the way suggested by Leibniz. His aim is to overcome the mind/matter dualism (the 'bifurcation of nature') that has plagued modern thought since Descartes. The best way to do this is not by privileging mind over matter, as the metaphysical idealists or mentalists do, he argues, but to elaborate a novel conception in which matter and mind are viewed as mutually correlated dimensions of a single event. 'The world,' Whitehead says in *Adventures of Ideas*, 'is not merely physical, nor is it merely mental' (AI 190).

In Whitehead's view, the Cartesian notions of mind and matter must therefore be reinterpreted as referring to coexisting aspects of a concrete occurrence in nature. It would be wrong – in fact, it would be an instance of the fallacy of misplaced concreteness – to take any of these aspects for a genuine, independently existing reality. What this precisely means will be explained later on in Chapter 5. As will be shown, Whitehead will elaborate a daringly novel conception of the basic constituents of reality.

SCIENCE AGAINST COMMON SENSE: THE TURN TO PROCESS

All this is purely philosophical argument. As such, it would never make a successfully working science deviate from its course. But the greatest challenge to the ontology of scientific materialism, Whitehead contends in *Science and the Modern World*, does not come from philosophy, but from science itself. Because of his solid scientific education, Whitehead was able to appreciate that quantum theory and Einstein's theory of relativity required an extraordinary reorganisation of ordinary modes of thought. 'The new situation in the thought of today,' he observed, 'arises from the fact that scientific theory is outrunning common sense' (SMW 114). Science itself had already effected a drastic revision of its most basic concepts. And if such a revision had been possible in science, why should it be regarded as impossible in philosophy?

As Whitehead views things, orthodox scientific materialism is deeply indebted to the common-sense view of the world. The atoms are conceived on the model of the macroscopic things of everyday life, as permanent entities moving around in the two great containers of space and time. In Whitehead's interpretation, quantum theory forces us to renounce the notion of enduring things moving continuously along linear trajectories; the basic constituents of reality make 'jumps' (SMW 129) from one spatio-temporal location to another. This suggests that the ultimate particles are to be conceived as event-like, as *occurrences* rather than as *continuants*. Furthermore, the permanent features we observe do not have to be interpreted in terms of continuously existing entities, but in terms of a *reiteration* of fundamental patterns within successive, existentially *discontinuous* events:

> The discontinuities introduced by the quantum theory
> require revision of physical concepts in order to meet them.
> In particular . . . some theory of discontinuous existence is
> required. What is asked from such a theory, is that an orbit of
> an electron can be regarded as a series of detached positions,
> and not as a continuous line. (SMW 135)

Relativity theory compels us to rethink another main feature of the worldview of scientific materialism. Space and time are more closely tied than previously thought, eventually collapsing into a unified concept, *space-time*. Moreover, Whitehead goes on to argue, the theory of relativity points to an essential connection between space and time on the one hand, and the particular occurrences of nature on the other. Although this involves a significant – and therefore very difficult – departure from ordinary modes of thought, we must conceive of space and time as *abstractions* from the intricate texture of concrete natural events:

> The new relativity associates space and time with an intimacy not hitherto contemplated; and presupposes that their separation in concrete fact can be achieved by alternative modes of abstraction . . . But each mode of abstraction is yielding attention to something which is in nature; and thereby is isolating it for the purpose of contemplation. (SMW 118)

As against *substantivalism*, the Newtonian view of space and time as independent substances, Whitehead thus opts for *relationalism*, the concurrent Leibnizian view of space and time as derivative of a system of spatial and temporal relations among events.

What is the moral that philosophers have to draw from all this? Scientific materialism, Whitehead concludes, is 'entirely unsuited to the scientific situation at which we have now arrived' (SMW 17). Philosophers, he says, have neither to indulge in historical studies nor provide detailed but sterile analyses of isolated technical problems (PR xiv). They must learn to be intellectually bold again – and dare to engage in the construction of a new metaphysical scheme.

A FORGOTTEN QUESTION: THE NATURE OF PHYSICAL EXISTENCE

The relevance of the above considerations for the contemporary debate should be obvious, but it may nevertheless be useful to dwell on this explicitly. Consider how the mind–body problem is typically framed by contemporary analytic philosophers. On the assumption that the universe is composed of material particles ruled by strict deterministic laws, explain in what sense (if any) consciousness, freedom and mental causation exist.

In his book of 1984, *Mind in a Physical World*, Jaegwon Kim nicely illustrates this approach when he says that

> Giving an account of mental causation – in particular, explaining how it is possible for the mental to exercise causal influences in the physical world – has been one of the main preoccupations in the philosophy of mind over the past two decades.[9]

As this passage makes clear, the problem is to incorporate recalcitrant phenomena into a metaphysic – the materialistic worldview – *already assumed to be true*. What if the recalcitrant phenomena obstinately refuse incorporation?

That this is indeed the case is admitted by Kim himself. In an essay that he contributed to a book entitled *The Future for Philosophy* (2004), he writes that the qualitative aspects of consciousness cannot be physically reduced: 'Qualia,' he says, 'are "the mental residue" that cannot be accommodated within the physical domain.'[10] Strangely enough, this does not lead him to cast materialism into doubt, apparently on the ground that 'there seems [to be] no credible alternative to physicalism as a general worldview'.[11] But of course we will never develop such an alternative if we do not even begin searching for one.

Descartes observes in the *Discourse on Method* (1637) that it is wiser to try to change the order of thought than the order of things. In issues of theoretical and practical concern, it is a sensible policy to re-examine one's own assumptions in the face of repeated failure to achieve one's goal. This is what Whitehead (and many contemporary philosophers, most notably perhaps Thomas Nagel and Galen Strawson) suggests we should do. Whether or not he is right in contending that experience is a fundamental feature of all things, he is certainly right in reminding us that the universe may be quite different from how the current philosophical consensus *assumes* it to be.

It may be tempting at this point to say that giving up the materialistic framework is tantamount to giving up the game. But this is precisely the point at issue: what reasons do we have for playing *that* game in the first place? Strangely enough, the materialistic framework seems to be accepted as a matter of course, as if it were an immediate fact of our experience or a scientific theory, rather than just one among many other metaphysical views. According to an influential author, Colin McGinn, 'it is consciousness that cries out for naturalistic explanation, not cerebral matter. Consciousness is the anomalous thing, the thing that tests our naturalistic view of the world.'[12] Is consciousness really such an anomalous thing? Thinkers of earlier generations felt that the perspective had to be reversed; for philosophers like Leibniz and Whitehead it was matter (not conscious experience) that 'cried out' for an explanation.

What is the nature of physical existence? This is a fundamental question and Whitehead has many puzzling yet deeply interesting things to say as an answer to it. Or so, at least, will be argued in what follows.

NOTES

1. The concept is discussed in P. F. Strawson, *Individuals: An Essay in Descriptive Metaphysics*, London and New York: Routledge, 1959, pp. 38–58.
2. For an insightful discussion of Spinoza's parallelism, see Michael Della Rocca, *Spinoza*, London and New York: Routledge, 2008, pp. 100–4.
3. One recent author who recognises the importance of the Principle of Sufficient Reason is Thomas Nagel. He is less cautious than Whitehead, however, for he reads it as straightforwardly incorporating a metaphysical truth. As he puts it: 'The view that rational intelligibility is at the root of the natural order makes me, in a broad sense, an idealist – not a subjective idealist, since it doesn't amount to the claim that all reality is ultimately appearance – but an objective idealist in the tradition of Plato . . . I suspect that there must be a strain of this kind of idealism in every theoretical scientist: pure empiricism is not enough' (*Mind and Cosmos: Why the Materialist Neo-Darwinian Conception of Nature is Almost Certainly False*, Oxford: Oxford University Press, p. 17). Can such a radical form of rationalism satisfy its own very strict intelligibility requirement? What makes it intelligible that reality shall have an intelligible structure?
4. A particularly strong version of the argument for panpsychism based upon the heterogeneity problem has been provided by Galen Strawson in 'Realistic Monism: Why Physicalism Entails Panpsychism', in A. Freeman (ed.), *Consciousness and its Place in Nature*, Exeter: Imprint Academic, 2006, pp. 3–31.

5. As John Searle contends in *Mind: A Brief Introduction*, Oxford: Oxford University Press, 2004, pp. 149–50. Even authors otherwise very appreciative of Whitehead's philosophy reject this aspect of his thought. A notable example is Peter Simons, 'The Seeds of Experience', in A. Freeman (ed.), *Consciousness and its Place in Nature*, Exeter: Imprint Academic, 2006, pp. 146–50.
6. David Skrbina's extended historical survey (*Panpsychism in the West*, Cambridge, MA: MIT Press, 2005) amply vindicates this claim of Whitehead by showing that panpsychism has been a major theme throughout Western philosophy. See also D. Skrbina (ed.), *Mind that Abides: Panpsychism in the New Millennium*, Amsterdam and Philadelphia: John Benjamins, 2009.
7. This is a condensed version of what is nowadays called 'the intrinsic nature argument' for panpsychism. D. Chalmers discusses it briefly in *The Conscious Mind* (Oxford: Oxford University Press, pp. 153–6): 'After all,' he writes there (echoing not solely Whitehead, but also Russell and James), 'we really have no idea about the intrinsic properties of the physical. Their nature is up for grabs, and phenomenal properties seem as likely a candidate as any other' (p. 154). This line of reasoning is discussed by W. Seager in 'The Intrinsic Nature Argument for Panpsychism', in A. Freeman (ed.), *Consciousness and its Place in Nature*, Exeter: Imprint Academic, 2006, pp. 129–45.
8. For an extended discussion of this longstanding interpretative question, see P. Phemister, *Leibniz and the Natural World. Activity, Passivity and Corporeal Substances in Leibniz's Philosophy*, Dordrecht: Springer, 2005.
9. J. Kim, *Mind in a Physical World: An Essay on the Mind–Body Problem and Mental Causation*, Cambridge, MA: MIT Press, 1998, p. 29
10. J. Kim, 'The Mind–Body Problem at Century's Turn', in B. Leiter (ed.), *The Future for Philosophy*, Oxford: Clarendon Press, 2004, p. 143.
11. Ibid., p. 146.
12. C. McGinn, *The Problem of Consciousness*, Oxford: Basil Blackwell, 1991, p. 69.

CHAPTER 2

Speculative Metaphysics: Defining the Ideal

THE LOGIC OF METAPHYSICAL THINKING

At the beginning of *Process and Reality*, Whitehead writes:

> This course of lectures is designed as an essay in Speculative Philosophy. Its task must be to define 'speculative' philosophy,' and to defend it as a method productive of important knowledge. (PR 3)

This is easier said than done. How is one to proceed in the formulation of such a scheme? At what kind of intellectual construction does the metaphysician precisely aim? Abandoning common sense (and ordinary language) is a potentially risky enterprise. Once the safe boundaries of ordinary thought are trespassed, one may easily end up talking nonsense or get lost in idle speculations. Whitehead was aware of this risk:

> Speculative boldness must be balanced by complete humility before logic, and before fact. It is a disease of philosophy when it is neither bold nor humble, but merely a reflection of the temperamental presuppositions of exceptional personalities. (PR 17)

Accordingly, the very first chapter of *Process and Reality* attempts to regiment revisionary thought by defining the methods, the aims and the criteria of success for speculative metaphysics.

Whitehead denies, to begin with, that a metaphysical theory can take the form of an axiomatic system. Neither the basic axioms nor the metaphysical notions used in framing them are given us from the start. How we have to think about reality cannot possibly be something we know *ab initio*; unless we are endowed with innate knowledge and notions (which Whitehead assumes not to be the case), basic principles and concepts can only be reached at the end of metaphysical research. 'Philosophy,' Whitehead says, 'has been misled by the example of mathematics' (PR 8); its deductive, foundational methods cannot be taken over in metaphysics. Always sensitive to the problems posed by language, he also remarks that at an early stage we lack not solely the 'axiomatic certainties from which to start. There is not even the language in which to frame them' (PR 13). 'A precise language,' he also explains, 'must await a completed metaphysical knowledge' (PR 12).

As the previous discussion of Whitehead's critique of scientific materialism in *Science and the Modern World* should have made clear, Whitehead conceives of metaphysics as being continuous with the natural sciences. It differs from them because of the wider scope of the experiences it seeks to explain and of the utmost generality of the notions it aims at. Its logic of discovery, however, is the same. Metaphysical schemes are giant scientific hypotheses to be tested against the bedrock of experienced reality. In *Process and Reality* the point is made thus:

> The true method of discovery is like the flight of an aeroplane. It starts from the ground of particular observation; it makes a flight in the thin air of imaginative generalization; and it again lands for renewed observation rendered acute by rational interpretation. (PR 5)

As he also has it:

> The use of such a matrix [a metaphysical scheme, that is, a system of basic concepts and principles] is to argue from it boldly and with rigid logic. The scheme should therefore be stated with the utmost precision and definiteness, to allow of such argumentation. The conclusion of the argument should then be confronted with circumstances to which it should apply. (PR 9)

Whitehead does not name the American philosopher and logician Charles Sanders Peirce in this context, but it is not difficult to discern in such an account the three crucial steps of *abduction* (hypothesis formation), *deduction* (derivation of testable consequences) and *induction* (the actual testing) that he had identified as constitutive of the method of all successful scientific inquiry.[1]

The first moment – the 'flight in the thin air of imaginative generalization' – particularly fascinated Peirce. How is it possible for the human mind to develop hypotheses that turn out to be true for at least some regions of reality, as the progress made in the sciences unequivocally shows? Peirce answered the question by reference to a doctrine of *cosmic attunement*. Human beings and the physical world have a common evolutionary history. In this process, the basic structures of our mind have been shaped by the basic structures of reality. This is what enables the scientist to make plausible guesses about the nature of the physical world.

Whitehead is also struck by the fact that human beings are capable of flashes of insight leading to the 'imaginative elaboration' (PR 9) of radically new conceptual schemes. But he says little to account for the phenomenon. What is clear is that Peirce's explanation is not one he would have gladly accepted. The basic categories of the human mind have indeed evolved, but in the wrong direction, namely on the basis of our dealings with the macroscopic things of everyday life. This does not lead to a better understanding of reality, but to that Aristotelian view of the world in which enduring things have ontological priority over events. (Eventually, it should be noted in passing, it is Whitehead's belief that our categories have an evolutionary origin that enables him to argue that they are *plastic* and therefore, at least in principle, revisable.)

Whitehead's scientific conception of metaphysics involves the abandonment of the quest for certainty that is typical of the Cartesian rationalist tradition. Metaphysical hypotheses are acceptable only as long as they are verified. The possibility that they may be falsified and that we have to reframe them anew is always open. At any one stage there could even be a plurality of systems with equal systematic elegance and comparable explanatory power. As Whitehead conceives of it, metaphysics is an open-ended, fallible enterprise. It is as much in process as the realities it seeks to grasp.

This notion immediately raises the question as to what kinds of experiences are relevant for testing a philosophical scheme. Whitehead's concept of experience includes not solely the observational laboratory experiences of the scientists or the ordinary sensory experiences of humankind. It also embraces our awareness of moral, aesthetic and religious values. Only by taking such experiences into account, Whitehead (rightly) contends, can we hope to achieve a genuinely synoptic vision of the nature of things. Whitehead's conception of metaphysics is therefore a very demanding one. The system he is aiming at must not only be able to unify different scientific theories such as quantum theory and relativity theory. It must also provide a synthesis of science and religion. Philosophy, he claims, 'attains its chief importance by fusing the two, namely, religion and science, into one rational scheme of thought' (PR 15).

Peirce understood modern science as a cooperative social enterprise aiming at universally agreed theories. The true theory of reality would be the one that all members of an ideal community of researchers would recognise as such in the long run. Not that he believed that agreement would be reached at some definite future time. That envisioned state was rather conceived by him as a Kantian regulative ideal – a projected end that propelled all sciences forward and kept them alive, unsatisfied with fragmentary results. This universal consensus among thinkers conceived as incarnations of pure rationality, however, cannot be achieved even in principle if, as Whitehead holds, our moral, aesthetic and religious experiences are also to be taken into account. Such experiences are not inter-subjectively available in the way in which scientific experiences are; they vary sensibly from person to person. People of a certain kind of psychological temperament may even want to deny that they have any religious experiences at all. In sum, even if conceived as firmly anchored in the empirical sciences, speculative metaphysics as Whitehead defines it remains an individual, private quest for meaning and truth.

A DISCIPLINE FOR THOUGHT: FOUR CRITERIA

In spite of this, there should be no arbitrariness in metaphysical concepts-formation, or at least it should be carefully checked and reduced to a minimum. In *Adventures of Ideas*, Whitehead writes:

Speculative Philosophy can be defined as the endeavour to frame a coherent, logical, necessary system of general ideas in terms of which every element of our experience can be interpreted. (AI 222)

In a similar passage from *Process and Reality*, Whitehead more clearly specifies the four criteria[2] that any metaphysical system should be able to satisfy. The ideal 'philosophical scheme,' he says, 'should be coherent, logical, and, in respect to its interpretation, applicable and adequate' (PR 3). These passages require some elucidation before they can be properly understood.

1. First, it should be noted that Whitehead's use of the word *coherence* is misleading. The term does not mean logical consistency (this notion is not rejected, but included in the second criterion). Ideally, metaphysical notions shall be such as to *require* each other, much in the way in which the concept of 'right' requires the concept of 'left'. The speculative mind cannot rest satisfied with a mere assemblage of concepts: 'It is the ideal of speculative philosophy that its fundamental notions shall not seem capable of abstraction from each other' (PR 3).

2. Secondly, Whitehead requires that each system shall be *logical*. This means that it must be consistent ('logically coherent') as well as incorporating the basic principles of deductive inference; this is needed in order for the system to have empirically testable consequences. The basic notions must also be arrived at by means of logically sound procedures: 'The term "logical",' Whitehead explains, 'has its ordinary meaning, including "logical" consistency, or lack of contradiction, the definition of constructs in logical terms, the exemplification of general logical notions in specific instances, and the principles of inference' (PR 3).

The other two criteria have to do with the empirical as opposed to the rational side of metaphysical inquiry.

3. *Applicability* means that at least *some* experienced item can be interpreted in terms of the notions of the metaphysical scheme.

This requirement is easily secured if one makes sure to construct one's notions by way of abstraction/generalisation from some selected portion of experience.

4. *Adequacy* means that *all* experienced items must be eventually interpreted in terms of the scheme. Obviously enough, this requirement is much more difficult to satisfy. Notions that were originally developed to make sense of a limited sphere must be able to account for regions not previously considered. Adequacy, one could say, is *universally extended applicability*: 'The success of the imaginative experiment is always to be tested by the applicability of its results beyond the restricted locus from which it originated' (PR 5).

One of the main uses of this list is to provide a basis for philosophical criticism. More precisely, each of these criteria provides a standard in terms of which to evaluate the viability of a conceptual scheme. As such, the list is not a pedantic exercise on the part of Whitehead, but constitutes an indispensable 'working tool' for the speculative metaphysician. Consider, for example, the critique of scientific materialism discussed in the previous chapter. The materialistic worldview, considered as such, is adequate to the interpretation of some selected portions of experience. Its notions, however, fail to apply to the phenomena of life and mind. De facto, the theory is rejected because it violates (4), the criterion of *adequacy*.

Descartes's substance dualism, Whitehead also argues, is the example of a system that violates (1), the criterion of *coherence*. The system lacks the right sort of 'conceptual tightness', which is manifest in Descartes's definition of substance as that which 'requires nothing but itself in order to exist' (PR 6). In this way, the two basic concepts of his philosophy, the notion of a spiritual *res cogitans* and of a material *res extensa*, lose any internal relationship. This is a particularly obvious violation of this basic requirement. Sometimes the lamentable 'arbitrary disconnection of first principles' (PR 6) may be more difficult to spot. Spinoza, for instance, avoids the problem of the Cartesian philosophy by acknowledging the reality of only one substance. Still, he makes himself guilty of an analogous error when he introduces the concept of the 'mode' as a manifestation of substance. On Spinoza's

(Cartesian) definition of substance – 'by substance I understand what is in itself and is conceived through itself', one reads in his *Ethics* – there is no reason whatsoever why a substance should make itself manifest at all. The modes are introduced to save the experience of there being a plurality of things, not because they are conceptually required by the definition of substance (cf. PR 6–7).

These are well-known objections against the systems of Descartes and Spinoza: what about Leibniz? In what sense can his system be said to be 'incoherent'? Some subtlety is involved with Whitehead's answer to this question. Another interesting application of the criterion of coherence is that it can be used to ground Occam's razor, the methodological principle according to which the less ontologically loaded explanation is to be preferred: *entia non sunt multiplicanda sine necessitate*. The more kinds of entities we introduce in our ontology, the greater the danger that they will make little intrinsic contact with one another. More dramatically, if the postulated entities are radically different in kind, then they will not be able to be intrinsically related in the strong way required by the criterion of coherence. Accordingly, we find Whitehead opting for ontological *type*-monism in *Process and Reality*, the view that all basic constituents of reality are identical in fundamental nature. (This is not to be confused with *number*-monism, the view that there is only one 'thing'.)

Another way to make the point that all basic entities are identical in fundamental nature is to say that they are all subject to the same basic ontological principles. Now, Whitehead observes, Leibniz argues that all monads are causally insulated from one another. There is one monad, however, for which this limitation does not hold, namely God. For surely, Whitehead reasons, Leibniz's *omnipotent* God must have the power to alter the nature of the created monads. As Whitehead has it, in Leibniz's system 'no reason can be given why the supreme monad, God, is exempted from the common fate of isolation' (AI 134). This sounds like an argument against the introduction of God within one's metaphysics. In truth, the reasoning only entails that, *if* there is a supreme entity, *then* it will have to be conceived on the same principles on which all other basic entities are conceived: 'God is not to be treated as an exception to all metaphysical principles, invoked to save their collapse. He is their chief exemplification' (PR 343). It remains to be seen, of course, whether Whitehead's own alternative metaphysics will be able to avoid the mistakes he imputes to the great rationalists of the past.

Another aspect of Whitehead's discussion of the criteria deserves recognition, especially because it so much conflicts with the mentality of contemporary analytic philosophers. This is Whitehead's downplaying of the intrinsic significance of logical consistency. In a passage in which Whitehead is probably meditating upon his experience as a mathematician, he comments upon the relative importance of logical consistency as follows:

> logical contradictions, except as temporary slips of the mind – plentiful, though temporary – are the most gratuitous of errors; and usually they are trivial. Thus, after criticism, systems do not exhibit mere illogicalities. They suffer from inadequacy and incoherence. (PR 6)

But it is not even coherence that we must first look for when assessing a new system (PR 6), Whitehead believes. What we must consider first in a philosophy – and learn to *value* – is whether it opens a new perspective upon the world and our place in it. Only a theory of this kind generates interest, keeps curiosity alive, in short, makes us feel involved in a real adventure, which is required to gain any genuinely new insight. This means that the dialectical method so much in vogue among analytic philosophers (at the time of Whitehead's writings, made popular by highly influential thinkers like G. E. Moore) of refuting a philosophical thesis *p* by showing that it entails a contradiction can only play a subordinate role in metaphysics. The sterility of the procedure is evident; the only conclusion we are entitled to draw on this basis, *not-p*, has no positive content and therefore adds little to our understanding of the world.

THE CONCEPT OF RATIONALITY: WHITEHEAD VS. LEIBNIZ

In *Science and the Modern World* Whitehead criticises the early modern scientists for their refusal to deal with ultimate metaphysical questions. In this connection, he discerns a deep meaning in the violent death of the Renaissance thinker Giordano Bruno. This occurred just before the rise of modern science:

Giordano Bruno was the martyr: though the cause for which
he suffered was not that of science, but that of free imaginative
speculation. His death in the year 1600 ushered in the first
century of modern science in the strict sense of the term. In
his execution there was an unconscious symbolism: for the
subsequent tone of scientific thought has contained distrust of
his type of general speculativeness. (SMW 1)

But how far is Whitehead himself prepared to go in this respect? What
limitations are set by his conception of metaphysics to the free play
of imaginative speculation? One way to answer these questions is by
comparing Whitehead's conception of rationality, as this is formulated
in the criteria (1) and (2), with the characterisation one finds in the
works of Leibniz. Other thinkers could have provided good examples
as well (Spinoza for instance), but Leibniz's formulations have the
advantage of being short and to the point. In the *Monadology*, for
example, he writes:

> Our reasonings are based on *two great principles, that of
> contradiction*, in virtue of which we judge that which involves
> a contradiction to be false, and that which is opposed or
> contradictory to the false to be true. And that of *sufficient
> reason*, by virtue of which we consider that we can find no
> true or existent fact, no true assertion, without there being a
> sufficient reason why it is thus and not otherwise, although
> most of the time these reasons cannot be known to us.
> (AG 217, §§31–2)

As Aristotle noticed in his *Metaphysics*, the man who violates the Principle of Contradiction is reduced to the level of a plant; de facto, he is not a rational being any more. The Principle of Sufficient Reason does not involve an analogous breakdown of rationality. The principle is violated when one arbitrarily stops searching for explanations – that is to say, when one refuses to go on asking *Why?* In this case, one does not step outside the realm of reason altogether; one does, however, fail to fulfil the ideal of a perfect rationality.

What is the status of these two principles within Whitehead's account of the nature of speculative metaphysics? The Principle of Contradiction is incorporated within Whitehead's criterion of coherence (2), while the

Principle of Sufficient Reason is not apparently included in any of the above criteria. This is surprising for, as argued in the previous chapter, Whitehead implicitly appeals to it in his critique of scientific materialism as incapable of explaining the existence of mind. The Principle of Sufficient Reason has a parallel, however, in what Whitehead calls 'the ontological principle'. In its canonical formulation, this runs as follows:

> the reasons for things are always to be found in the composite nature of definite actual entities . . . The ontological principle can be summarized as: no actual entity, then no reason. (PR 19)

Alternatively, and more clearly, Whitehead writes:

> This ontological principle means that actual entities are the only *reasons*; so that to search for a *reason* is to search for one or more actual entities. (PR 24)

Given that actual entities are the basic constituents of the natural world, Whitehead is here de facto replacing Leibniz's (stronger) *nihil est sine ratione* with the (weaker) *nihil est sine causa*. On this reading, to provide an 'explanation' of a thing is to reconstruct its genesis by displaying the way in which one or more causes worked together in bringing it about. But what about asking why that causal series exists at all? This question cannot be legitimately posed within the framework set by Whitehead's four criteria. A metaphysics whose methods are modelled on the example of the natural sciences can only provide an interpretation of the inner structure and workings of the experienced world. The existence of that world is a primordial 'datum' to be acknowledged as such.

As a matter of fact, we never find Whitehead raising the question that so much fascinated Leibniz in *The Principles of Nature and Grace, Based on Reason* (1714), why there is something rather than nothing (AG 208, §7). This may be sound methodology. Given that absolute non-existence is not a self-contradictory notion, however, there is a real issue here that Whitehead fails to address. Why is it not the case that nothing exists? The question may be unanswerable in the end; but in his search for 'ultimate meanings', Whitehead is certainly not as radical as his great German forerunner.

METAPHYSICS VINDICATED

Over the last century, metaphysics has been the target of many virulent attacks. Neo-Kantians have depicted it as an illegitimate violation of the bounds of human cognition. Wittgensteinians and neo-positivists have charged it with literal insignificance, a metaphysician's solemn pronouncements having only the appearance of being meaningful statements. Relativists have denied the possibility of there being any Truth at all, be it of a metaphysical or any other kind. Lastly, naturalised ontologists *à la* Quine have argued that science provides all the metaphysical knowledge we both need and can possibly achieve; as he forcefully put it in an often quoted passage, 'philosophy of science is philosophy enough'.[3]

In the end, however, none of these attempts has turned out to be successful. In part, they are based upon questionable assumptions. Is it so obvious that science is the only source of reliable knowledge given that, as Whitehead pointed out, it discards so much of our human experience? In part, such attacks are bluntly self-refuting. The neo-Kantian notion that there can be knowledge only of empirical things is offered as a piece of 'transcendental', that is to say, non-empirical, knowledge. Analogously, the neo-positivist doctrine that only empirically verifiable statements are meaningful is not itself verifiable. Finally, the relativistic claim that there are no truths entails its own falsity.

Is there anything now that can be said against Whitehead's conception of an 'empirical metaphysics', as it could be called? This question must be answered in the negative. Not everyone will have an interest in it, of course, nor is there any obligation for anyone to actually pursue it. Nevertheless, Whitehead's careful definition vindicates it as a fully legitimate area of theoretical investigation. As he rightly argued almost a century ago, 'metaphysics' (if properly understood) need not be a word of contempt.

NOTES

1. See especially C. S. Peirce, 'Deduction, Induction and Hypothesis', *Popular Science Monthly* 13, 1878, pp. 470–82.

2. A longer, still tentative list of criteria 'to which the content of a belief should be subjected' is provided by Whitehead in *The Function of Reason* (1929), Boston: Beacon Press, 1958, pp. 67–8.
3. W. v. O. Quine, 'Mr. Strawson on Logical Theory', *Mind* 62, 1953, p. 446.

PART II

From Permanence to Process

CHAPTER 3

Deconstructing Tradition: Substance Revisited

THE MEANING OF SUBSTANCE

The label 'metaphysics of process' is sometimes used in antithesis to 'metaphysics of substance'.[1] This is not mistaken, but inaccurate. The term 'substance' has been used in a variety of meanings in the history of philosophy. Specifically, the term has been used to designate all of the following (the list is not meant to be exhaustive):

1. That which truly *is*.
2. That which is capable of action.
3. That which is always a subject of predication and never a predicate.
4. The underlying bearer of properties.
5. That which remains identical throughout change.
6. That which requires nothing else in order to exist.
7. That which is simple (that is, no substance has parts that are themselves substances).
8. That which is not affected from without.[2]

In his account of the nature of the ultimate building blocks of reality, Whitehead retains the meanings (1) and (2), but rejects all others: the basic substances are power-units of sorts, capable of both acting and being acted upon. This is, he thinks, Plato's teaching in the *Sophist*. In *Adventures of Ideas* he first quotes a passage from Benjamin Jowett's translation of this crucial dialogue:

> My suggestion would be, that anything which possesses any sort of power to affect another, or to be affected by another even for a moment, however trifling the cause and however slight and momentary the effect, has real existence; and I hold that the definition of being is simply power. (*Sophist*, 247, as quoted in AI 119)

Then, he comments on it as follows:

> Plato says that it is the *definition* of being that it exert power and be subject to the exertion of power. This means that the essence of being is to be implicated in causal action on other beings . . . Plato enunciates the doctrine that 'action and reaction' belong to the essence of being. (AI 119–20)

The rejected notions (3)–(8), all of which can be traced back, either directly or indirectly, to Aristotle's *Categories*, are systematically connected. The logical notion of a substance as a subject of predication (3) has its immediate counterpart in the ontological conception of a substance as a bearer of properties (4). On this basis, to say that a thing 'changes' can only mean that there is something in it, the substance conceived as an underlying substratum, which remains identical in the midst of the thing's shifting attributes (5). Finally, conceived as a substratum, the substance enters into relation only with its properties. This makes it easy to think of substance as something primary, that is, as needing no other substance in order to exist (6), and therefore also as simple, that is, not constituted by any other substance (7), and therefore also as incapable of being altered in its internal constitution (8). Cumulatively, these Aristotelian notions support the theory that a substance is something static and inert, as well as independent from any other substances.[3]

This account is hardly to be made consistent with the conception expressed in (2), according to which substances are inherently active beings. Since Whitehead not solely retains, but even stresses the importance of the dynamic concept, it would be wrong to say that his process metaphysics involves a wholesale rejection of the category of substance; he simply wants to purify it from its spurious elements. Whitehead argues in *Process and Reality* that these two ways of conceiving of substance, in his view the 'Platonic' and the 'Aristotelian', coexist within all the great philosophical systems of modern time. But it is in the philosophy of Leibniz, he believes, that the contradiction between them has achieved its clearest – and most productive – manifestation.

THE METAPHYSICS OF SUBSTANCE

Whitehead is not alone in this estimate. One book that had a lasting impact upon his philosophical development was Russell's *A Critical Exposition of the Philosophy of Leibniz* (1900).[4] Here as in many other writings, Russell denounces the metaphysical inadequacy of substance-property ontology. On this basis, he contends, only two main types of metaphysical systems can be constructed. One is Leibniz's theory of a plurality of independent monads, the other Spinoza's theory of a single encompassing Reality. Since both theories are plainly false, Russell concludes, the metaphysician has to reject substance-property ontology.

Russell makes the point thus:

> Spinoza, we may say, had shown that the actual world could not be explained by means of one substance; Leibniz showed that it could not be explained by means of many substances. It became necessary, therefore, to base metaphysics *on some notion other than that of substance* – a task not yet accomplished. (PL 126; my emphasis)

This is a striking passage. What else could the *notion other than that of substance* be if not the notion of *event*?

Whitehead repeats the argument in a number of places, for example in *The Concept of Nature*:

> Some schools of philosophy, under the influence of the Aristotelian logic and the Aristotelian philosophy, endeavour to get on without admitting any relations at all except that of substance and attribute. Namely all apparent relations are to be resolvable into the concurrent existence of substances with contrasted attributes. It is fairly obvious that the Leibnizian monadology is the necessary outcome of any such philosophy. If you dislike pluralism, there will be only one monad. (CN 150)

The argument is more complex than it may look at first sight; it may briefly be stated thus:

1. Relations cannot be analysed in terms of the concepts of substance and property. (Thesis shared by Russell and Whitehead.)
2. Hence, if the ultimate constituents of things are bearers of properties, relations are to be condemned as unreal. This means that the metaphysician will have to eliminate them from his worldview.
3. On this basis, the world can be conceived either as a single Substance (in the way of Spinoza) or as a plurality of unrelated substances (in the way of Leibniz).
4. Since both these metaphysical theories (Spinoza's monism and Leibniz's pluralism) are patently absurd, the doctrine that only substrata and their properties are real must be rejected as false.

In his several discussions of this argument, Russell is especially concerned with grounding premise (1).[5] Consider the statement 'A is higher than B.' It would seem natural to analyse it in terms of the conjunction 'A is of height X' and 'B is of height Y.' In this way, one may hold, relations are shown to be unnecessary. As against this, Russell contends that the purported analysis of that statement is incomplete unless one also specifies that X *is greater than* Y; in this way, however, appeal is made once again to the category of relation. This immediately leads to step (2) of the argument. Since relations cannot be accommodated within the substance-quality paradigm, the metaphysician who is not willing to cast that paradigm into question has no other option than to deny their ultimate reality.

Thesis (2) also raises the question whether it is true to say that Leibniz denied that relations are real, for Leibniz does not say that they are 'unreal', but that they are 'ideal'. According to Russell, Leibniz saw that relations cannot be reduced to properties. Having gone so far, he should have acknowledged relations as among the basic constituents of reality. His obstinate belief in the subject–predicate logic prevented him from doing so. Torn between his own insights and his traditional Aristotelian background, he looked for a compromise solution. Hence he ended up arguing that relations are 'ideal' – that is to say, 'half-real' or 'semi-real'. For Russell, this is a subterfuge not worthy of a great logician.

With respect to (3), Russell observes that Leibniz's monadism and Spinoza's monism are not logically on a par, as only Spinoza's is a coherent form of substance metaphysics. Leibniz believes his monads to be components of the very same universe. But there is no way to make sense of the idea of their unity within one world without introducing the notion of their being related. In order to achieve unity without recourse to relations, Leibniz would have to reduce *all* monads to adjectives of a *single* Substance. In this way, he would have become himself a monist.

Did the concept of substance/substratum really play the role Russell ascribes to it in the philosophies of these two rationalists? This is doubtful. Logical considerations are important in Leibniz's *Discourse on Metaphysics*, but almost irrelevant in the *Monadology* and the *Principles of Nature and Grace*. Russell himself admits in his admirable study that in the correspondence with De Volder, Leibniz is on the verge of adopting a process conception of the monad, as this almost dissolves here into the mere series of its perceptual states.[6] As far as Spinoza is concerned, there is at least *prima facie* evidence for supposing that the answer must be negative as well. Spinoza has three basic categories (the triad 'substance–attribute–mode'), not just two. Moreover, neither the attributes nor the modes can be interpreted as qualities of an underlying substance; as Spinoza makes abundantly clear, they are not a substance's properties but (more intriguingly) its *expressions* or *manifestations*.[7]

THE PHENOMENOLOGY OF SUBSTANCE

But even if Russell were right, the argument would work as a *reductio* of the substance-predicate paradigm only if it were true that monadism and monism are absurd. Russell says little to justify this claim. Whitehead sees that this point stands in need of justification. What makes the metaphysics of Spinoza and Leibniz utterly incredible, he says, is that '[e]ither alternative stamps experience with a certain air of illusoriness' (PR 190).

A simpler rendering of the argument analysed in the previous section is as follows:

1. The only views of the world that can be articulated on the basis of a substance-predicate ontology are Leibniz's theory of unrelated substances or Spinoza's theory of a single Substance.

2. But these ways of explaining the world are absurd.
3. Hence, substance-predicate ontology must be rejected.

What kind of 'absurdity' is here at stake? Whitehead's charge has to be understood with reference to his analysis of experience. This involves a rejection of what he refers to as 'the sensationalist doctrine of perception'. Whitehead is convinced that we constantly perceive that there are *many things* around us (which, for him, rules out Monism) as well as that *they act upon us* in a multitude of ways (which, for him, rules out causally independent monads). In conversation with one of his Harvard colleagues, the point is made thus: '*Being tackled at Rugby, there is the Real*. Nobody who hasn't been knocked down has the slightest notion of what the Real is.'[8] In having such a violent experience we feel absolutely certain – with a vividness we cannot possibly resist – that there are independent causal powers taking hold of us.

Whitehead's view that we have a direct apprehension of external causal powers is, for once, also the view of common sense. Philosophically, however, it is a very bold one. After Hume's *Treatise*, philosophers have been accustomed to think of our experience of causal processes as a matter of experiencing a succession of distinct events. This may be the case when one observes two objects acting upon one another, as in Hume's favourite example of the two striking billiard balls. But things change radically when *we* ourselves are involved in the causal transaction. In these cases, we are able to observe the workings of causation from 'within'. This happens, for example, when a light makes a man blink: 'The man will explain his experience by saying, "The flash made me blink"; and if his statement be doubted, he will reply, "I know it, because I felt it"' (PR 175). Of course, we cannot expect to have a clear and distinct sensory image of such powers in the same way in which we have a clear and distinct sensation of red when we look at a red object. But for Whitehead this only shows that Hume's analysis of ordinary human experience in terms of sensory impressions is unduly narrow. The kind of experience we have when we fall on the ground or are violently beaten with some hard object can hardly be described as an apprehension of distinct sense-impressions.

These considerations led Whitehead to draw a distinction between two experiential modes, respectively termed 'perception in the mode of causal efficacy' and 'perception in the mode of presentational immediacy'. At times, one of the modes predominates over the other. The perception of causal forces is stronger in the dark, when we feel at the mercy of unseen external agents. When we are mentally tired or depressed, on the contrary, the world reduces to a dull show of meaningless sensations. Ordinarily, the two modes coexist. Our total field of consciousness at any one moment includes a central nucleus of clear and distinct perceptions, as well as a penumbral area of vague, confused, emotionally charged ones:

> [Perception in the mode of causal efficacy] produces percepta which are vague, not to be controlled, heavy with emotion: it produces the sense of derivation from an immediate past, and of passage to an immediate future; a sense of emotional feeling, belonging to oneself in the past, passing into oneself in the present, and passing from oneself in the present towards oneself in the future; a sense of influx of influence from other vague presences in the past, localized and yet evading local definition, such influence modifying, enhancing, inhibiting, diverting, the stream of feeling which we are receiving, unifying, enjoying, and transmitting. This is our general sense of existence, as one item among others, in an efficacious actual world . . .
>
> The percepta in the mode of presentational immediacy have the converse characteristics. In comparison, they are distinct, definite, controllable, apt for immediate enjoyment, and with the minimum of reference to past, or to future. (PR 178–9)

As Whitehead views things, traditional empiricism has disregarded the rich sensuous background, systematically neglecting all that is chaotic and vague in our experience. That there is more to our awareness of the world than clear-cut sensations is, of course, a major theme in James's philosophy of mind.[9] As he writes in *The Principles of Psychology*:

> It is . . . the re-instatement of the vague to its proper place in our mental life which I am so anxious to press on the attention . . . the definite images of traditional psychology form but the very smallest part of our minds as they actually live. The traditional psychology talks like one who should say a river consists of nothing but pailsful, spoonsful, quartpostful, barrelful, and other moulded forms of water. Even were the pails and the pots all actually standing in the stream, still

> between them the free water would continue to flow. It is just this free water of consciousness that psychologists resolutely overlook. Every definite image in the mind is steeped and dyed in the free water that flows round it. With it goes the sense of its relations, near and remote, the dying echo of whence it came to us, the dawning sense of wither it is to lead. (PP 254–5)

For James, the greatest sinners in this respect are Berkeley and Hume, whose 'ridiculous theory' is that 'we can have no images but of perfectly definite things' (PP 254). In their account of a moment of human mentality as a 'collection' or 'bundle' of distinct perceptions, these two thinkers are concealed rationalists with a bias for what is clear and distinct, not open-minded empiricists. Whitehead makes pretty much the same point when he says that 'Locke's successors, who arrogated to themselves the title of "empiricists," have been chiefly employed in explaining away the obvious facts of experience in obedience to the *a priori doctrine of sensationalism*' (PR 145, my emphasis).

How does an understanding of Whitehead's theory of experience – and especially his account of experiences of causal powers – help us to understand the charge of absurdity that he raises against the metaphysics of Leibniz and Spinoza? Now, it is difficult to deny that there is a dynamic dimension to our experience that traditional empiricist theories fail to do justice to. Whitehead is right when he insists that experience is not just a matter of *looking* at things, but also of *acting* and *being acted upon* – he does well to remind us that we are not mere spectators, but *doers* as well.

Still, appealing to experiences of causal efficacy as a way of refuting Leibniz's doctrine of the causal insulation of the monads may appear argumentatively weak. Leibniz could easily grant that our experiences suggest causal efficacy, but at the same time refuse to admit that they bear witness to the existence of real causal connections. Analogously, the appeal to our experiences as a way of refuting Spinoza would seem to be quite ineffective. For Spinoza is not denying that there *are* many things around us. What he points out is that such things are to be viewed as *modes* of a larger encompassing Substance; he is not casting the very existence of external things into question, but simply trying to assess their status in terms of the basic ontological categories of his system.

It must be admitted that there is nothing in Whitehead's analysis of experience that is of the nature of a proof. Consequently, the best way to read his account is to take it as an earnest invitation to consider one's experiences more closely and decide for oneself which interpretation is the more appropriate. Looking at his theory in this way, it becomes hard to deny that his account is superior to traditional empiricist ones. Moreover, it also becomes plain that he is raising a very serious question. Given that ordinary experience inevitably *suggests* a constant apprehension of causal agencies, how could we ever *believe* Leibniz's doctrine of the unreality of causal interaction? And how could we ever persuade ourselves, as Spinoza holds, that the multifarious things around us are not true individuals, considering that we experience them as sources of power? In order to give full credence to these doctrines, we would have to silence our most natural epistemic instincts, which is certainly not an easy thing to do.

In terms of Whitehead's criteria, we have here a clear violation of the requirement of empirical adequacy. One of the most salient aspects of our ordinary experiences cannot be made sense of by the rationalist systems of Leibniz and Spinoza. More than this is involved in this critique, however, for the rejection of these systems entails that their philosophies are tinged with a note of insincerity. For Whitehead, metaphysical inquiry must produce more than nice objects of contemplation; what we need are theories we can also live by.

THE EPISTEMOLOGY OF SUBSTANCE

In *Process and Reality*, Whitehead deepens his critique of the substance-predicate mode of thought by providing an epistemological version of the above argument against the metaphysics of substance. If the relation between the perceiving subject and the perceived object is interpreted in terms of the substance-quality paradigm, he argues, then all one obtains are two isolated entities, qualified by their private properties, yet unable to enter into that living, dynamic relation in which the having of an experience consists.

Of the shortcomings of Descartes's philosophy, Whitehead writes:

> It is quite obvious that the accidental relationships between
> diverse individual substances form a great difficulty for

Descartes. If they are to be included in his scheme of the actual world, they must be qualities of a substance. Thus a relationship is the correlation of a pair of qualities, one belonging exclusively to one individual, and the other exclusively to the other individual. (PR 144)

This epistemologically revised argument against the notions of substance and property may be stated thus:

1. Relations cannot be analysed in terms of the concepts of substance and property.
2. Hence, if the subject of experience and the experienced object are conceived as substances, they turn out to be unable to make contact with one another.
3. On this basis, the subject can never be assured of the existence of an external world.
4. Since scepticism is patently absurd, the doctrine that only substrata and properties are real must be rejected.

Given what has been said so far, there is no need to discuss this argument in detail. Having an experience as simple as burning one's finger already provides for Whitehead all the evidence of the existence of other things one can possibly ask for. You can subtly debate sceptical questions if you want to, but this is just a way of wasting your time – for in truth, you do not doubt at all.

The historical importance of Descartes's philosophy lies for Whitehead in the fact that it focused attention on the subject of experience. An alternative to the Aristotelian tradition that sees everyday objects as paradigmatic substances was thereby opened. Nevertheless, Whitehead thinks, Descartes badly misunderstood the significance of his own break with tradition. The paradox of Descartes's philosophy is that he divorced the subject from the material world, but at the same time continued to interpret it in terms of ontological categories derived from that world, as if the self were a 'thing'. Descartes should have discarded the old Aristotelian paradigm and carved new ontological categories from a fresh examination of the self. He discovered a potentially fruitful terrain for philosophical research, but failed to explore it:

> He [Descartes] . . . laid down the principle, that those substances which are the subjects enjoying conscious experiences provide the primary data for philosophy, namely, themselves as in the enjoyment of such experience. This is the famous subjectivist bias which entered into modern philosophy through Descartes. In this doctrine Descartes undoubtedly made the greatest philosophical discovery since the age of Plato and Aristotle . . . But like Columbus who never visited America, Descartes missed the full sweep of his own discovery . . . and continued to construe the functionings of the subjective enjoyment of experience according to the substance-quality categories. (PR 159)

In *Process and Reality*, Whitehead also illustrates this charge with respect to Descartes's celebrated argument that no meditator can possibly cast his or her own existence into doubt; as long as one doubts, one necessarily exists. But what is the exact content of this unquestionable truth? According to Whitehead, with every new instance of doubt a new self is present; hence, the *cogito* argument by itself does not suffice to justify belief in a permanent Self distinct from one's own thoughts. All that one can with certainty assert to exist at the moment of doubt is the existence of what may be called 'the momentary thought-occurrence'.

Whitehead formulates his critique as follows:

> In the quotation from the second *Meditation*: 'I am, I exist, is necessarily true each time that I pronounce it, or that I mentally conceive it,' Descartes adopts the position that an act of experience is the primary type of actual occasion. But in his subsequent developments he assumes that his mental substances endure change. Here he goes beyond his argument. For each time he pronounces 'I am, I exist,' the actual occasion, which is the ego, is different . . . (PR 75)

This is, among other things, a philosophically acute interpretation of one crucial episode in the history of modern philosophy. (The passage also anticipates some features of Whitehead's own theory of the self, to be discussed later on in Chapter 6, according to which it is nothing over and above the series of our momentary thought-occurrences.) But how just is it as a critique of the founder of modern philosophy?

Descartes does indeed conceive of the soul as some sort of enduring entity in the *Meditations*, but there is little evidence that he also conceives of it as a bearer of properties, as Whitehead would like to have it. A subject's thoughts (in the broad sense in which Descartes uses the term 'thought', so as to include not solely conceptual awareness, but also willing, imagining and perceiving) are hardly his qualities. The distinction between the soul and its attributes is better viewed as being a conceptual rather than a real one.[10] Cartesian 'thoughts' are the specific ways in which a subject exists over a given length of time, not properties standing in relation to a (mysterious) underlying and ontically distinct substance. Furthermore, it remains highly questionable whether the substance-predicate paradigm had the historical role Whitehead claims it had in generating the problem of scepticism. Descartes raises the sceptical question in the context of an attempt to reach a firm basis for our knowledge. But there is no evidence in the *Meditations* that he was also *induced* into posing it by his adherence to an inadequate ontological paradigm. (On the contrary, Descartes couldn't be clearer as to the fact that his sceptical doubts are only methodical.)

All in all, the impression one gets when considering Whitehead's critique is that he is trying to force Descartes's thinking into a preconceived interpretative grid rather than letting him speak with his own voice. Whitehead is not always consistent in his interpretation and evaluations of past philosophers, however; as will be shown in Chapter 6, he admits in *Adventures of Ideas* that there may be a closer proximity between his own theory of subjectivity and Descartes's.

TOWARDS A UNIFIED ACCOUNT OF SUBSTANCE

It is now time to turn to a more positive consideration of Whitehead's conception of substance. Again, the first question to be asked here is methodological: what entities are to be taken as paradigmatic? On what models is our conception of substance to be framed? A survey of Whitehead's metaphysical writings reveals that he is willing to consider more than one candidate:

1. Living organisms
2. Basic entities postulated by modern physical science
3. The subject of experience

The first approach takes biology and physiology as the fundamental sciences, the second and third give pride of place to physics and psychology, respectively. Apparently, all these sciences are regarded as legitimate starting points for metaphysical generalisation. Consider, for example, the following passage, in which all the approaches – the biological, the physical and the psychological – are mentioned at once:

> The philosophy of organism [Whitehead's own metaphysics], in its scheme for one type of actual entities, adopts the view that Locke's account of mental substances embodies, in a very special form, a more penetrating philosophic description than does Descartes's account of corporeal substance . . . On the whole, this is the moral to be drawn from the *Monadology* of Leibniz. His monads are best conceived as generalizations of contemporary notions of mentality. The contemporary notions of physical bodies only enter into his philosophy subordinately and derivatively. The philosophy of organism endeavours to hold the balance more evenly. (PR 19)

In *Science and the Modern World*, Whitehead writes:

> [T]he science of living organisms is only now coming to a growth adequate to impress its conceptions upon philosophy. (SMW 41)

At the same time, he also says in *Science and the Modern World* that as a matter of fact he first arrived at his basic ontological concepts by way of his study of physics rather than psychology; the two approaches, however, are not to be regarded as exclusive:

> It is equally possible to arrive at this organic conception of the world if we start from the fundamental notions of modern physics, instead of . . . from psychology and physiology. In fact by reason of my own studies in mathematics and mathematical physics, I did . . . arrive at my convictions in this way. (SMW 152)

What are we to make of all this? This variety of approaches may seem puzzling at first sight. It looks as if Whitehead had no clear idea as to where to begin his examination. This impression is to be resisted, however, for there are systematic reasons behind Whitehead's apparent (and only apparent) uncertainty.

As argued above, the metaphysician aims at a theory that will unify all the sciences while at the same time illuminating all the basic experiences of humankind. This means that the ultimate generalisations will have to be carved out patiently from different starting points. Conceptions derived from one science or from one realm of experience will have to be carefully balanced against one another, changed so as to be made mutually consistent, until they eventually converge into a few basic notions of the highest generality.

Unless this abstractive/comparative method is applied – Whitehead asks us to ponder – we will never be able to overcome one-sided dualisms such as that involved in the Cartesian bifurcation of nature into an intimately known realm of mind and an utterly extraneous realm of matter:

> any doctrine which refuses to place human experience outside nature, must find in descriptions of human experience factors which also enter into the descriptions of less specialized natural occurrences . . . We should either admit dualism, at least as a provisional doctrine, or we should point out the identical elements connecting human experience with physical science. (AI 184–5)

In working with different paradigms, Whitehead is simply following the logic inherent in his conception of metaphysics. Given the complexity of the enterprise, however, we cannot hope that his theory of substances – the ultimate building blocks of reality – will be an easy one to grasp.[11]

NOTES

1. Nicholas Rescher's excellent survey *Process Metaphysics: An Introduction to Process Philosophy*, Albany, NY: State University of New York Press, 1996, for instance, is entirely based upon such an opposition; see especially p. 35.

2. An analogous list is to be found in Peter Forrest, 'Sprigge's Spinoza', in P. Basile and L. McHenry (eds), *Consciousness, Reality and Value: Essays in Honour of T. L. S. Sprigge*, Frankfurt: Ontos Verlag, 2007, p. 136.
3. This understanding of substance, it should be noted, is the ontological counterpart of the atomistic materialism of modern science that Whitehead rejects.
4. I have argued for this point already in my *Leibniz, Whitehead and the Metaphysics of Causation*, Basingstoke and New York: Palgrave Macmillan, 2009, pp. 100–4.
5. This aspect of Russell's critical interpretation of Leibniz's philosophy has received much attention from commentators. See, for example, G. H. R. Parkinson, *Logic and Reality in Leibniz's Metaphysics*, Oxford: Clarendon Press, 1965; H. Ishiguro, 'Leibniz's Theory of the Ideality of Relations', in H. Frankfurt (ed.), *Leibniz: A Collection of Critical Essays*, New York: Anchor Books, 1972, pp. 191–224; B. Mates, *The Philosophy of Leibniz: Metaphysics and Language*, Oxford and New York: Oxford University Press, 1986; N. Rescher, 'Leibniz on Intermonadic Relations', in *On Leibniz*, Pittsburgh: University of Pittsburgh Press, 2003, pp. 68–91; M. Mugnai, *Leibniz's Theory of Relations*, Stuttgart: Meiner Verlag, 1992.
6. In a letter to De Volder, Leibniz speaks of the monad as 'something analogous to the soul, whose nature consists in a certain eternal law of the same series of change' (AG 173). A recent discussion of Leibniz's account of the relationship holding between a monad and the law determining the series of its changes is provided by J. Whipple, 'The Structure of Leibnizian Simple Substances', *British Journal for the History of Philosophy* 18/3, 2010, pp. 379–410.
7. These Spinozan concepts are further discussed from a process perspective in P. Basile, 'Russell on Spinoza's Substance Monism', *Metaphysica: International Journal for Ontology and Metaphysics* 13/1, 2012, pp. 27–41. For a Whiteheadian reading, see also Francesca di Poppa, 'Spinoza and Process Ontology', *The Southern Journal of Philosophy* 48/3, 2010, pp. 272–94.
8. W. E. Hocking, 'Whitehead as I Knew Him', in G. K. Kline (ed.), *Alfred North Whitehead: Essays on his Philosophy*, Englewood Cliffs, NJ: Prentice Hall, 1963, p. 15.

9. The (immense) influence of William James on Whitehead is explored in the last chapter of Marcus Ford, *William James's Philosophy: A New Perspective*, Amherst, MA: University of Massachusetts Press, 1982. Whitehead pays homage to James in *Modes of Thought*: 'His [James's] mind was adequately based upon the learning of the past. But the essence of his greatness was his marvelous sensitivity to the ideas of the present. He knew the world in which he lived, by travel, by personal relations with its leading men, by the variety of his own studies. He systematized; but above all he assembled. His intellectual life was one protest against the dismissal of experience in the interest of system' (MT 3).
10. This point is forcefully made by Galen Strawson in his discussion of Descartes's conception of the soul in *Selves: An Essay in Revisionary Metaphysics*, Oxford: Clarendon Press, 2009, p. 339.
11. Eventually, physics and psychology will play a greater role than biology in Whitehead's attempt at developing a new concept of substance. This is not surprising, as biology deals with entities of a high level of physical complexity.

CHAPTER 4

The Flowing Self: From Monads to Actual Occasions

WHITEHEAD ON THE SIGNIFICANCE OF LEIBNIZ'S THEORY OF MONADS

According to Whitehead, the thinker who came closest to formulating a correct account of substance is Leibniz. Whitehead praises him for the 'novelty of his monads' and for having seen that the ultimate substances must be 'processes of organization'. But the notion that they are 'windowless' – that is to say, causally insulated – cannot be accepted. Only a metaphysics that fully acknowledges the reality of causal interaction can account for our general sense of existence as being 'one item among others, in an efficacious actual world' (PR 178).

Whitehead does, of course, also praise Locke for his critique of the notion of substance/substratum and for his recognition of the fact that the notion of power is an essential ingredient in our understanding of substances. On the one hand, Locke observes in *An Essay Concerning Human Understanding* (1689), the notion of substance as a substratum of qualities is a rather empty one:

> if any one will examine himself concerning his *Notion of pure Substance in general*, he will find that he has no other *Idea* of it at all, but only a Supposition of he knows not what support of . . . Qualities.[1]

On the other hand, our ideas of particular things are essentially linked with our apprehension of the effect they are capable of bringing about.

Empirically considered, particular things are nothing but bundles of powers. As Locke makes the case with respect to our idea of a piece of gold:

> *Powers* . . . justly *make a great part of our complex* Ideas of Substances. He, that will examine his complex *Idea* of Gold, will find several of its *Ideas*, that make it up, to be only *Powers*, as the Power of being melted, but not spending it self in the Fire; of being dissolved in *Acqua Regia*, are *Ideas*, as necessary to make up our complex *Idea* of Gold, as its Colour and Weight: which if duly considered, are also nothing but different Powers. For to speak truly, Yellowness is not actually in Gold, but is a Power in Gold, to produce that *Idea* in us by our Eyes, when placed in a due Light . . .[2]

Whitehead is also fascinated by the openness of outlook generally displayed by Locke in his survey of the intricate texture of human experience (cf. PR 145). Nevertheless, as he justly remarks, Locke was essentially an epistemologist with no interest in metaphysics. The analyses in the *Essay* opened up a new horizon for metaphysical investigation, but it was Leibniz who began developing a new metaphysics of substance.

THE FUNDAMENTAL TENSION

Leibniz's descriptions of the monads in the *Monadology* are brief but suggestive. Each monad is a unique synthesis of perceptions (AG 214, §14); moreover, their inner life is ongoing activity (AG 214, §11), as each monad is driven by an inner desire (*appetition*) for novel experiences (AG 215, §15). Whitehead applauds this understanding of the monad as an experiential process-unit. 'Each monadic creature,' he remarks approvingly, 'is a mode of the process of "feeling" the world, of housing the world in one unit of complex feeling, in every way determinate' (PR 80). But of his own metaphysics, he also says:

> This is a theory of monads; but it differs from Leibniz's in that his monads change. In the organic theory, they merely *become*. (PR 80)

It is important to notice the point of distinguishing sharply between the concept of *change* and the concept of *becoming*. This highlights what Whitehead takes to be a fundamental tension in Leibniz's metaphysics. On the one hand, Leibniz's monads are mind-like currents of experience. On the other, Whitehead thinks, they are conceived by Leibniz in an Aristotelian fashion as substrata to which qualities inhere. On this view, monads 'change' – that is to say, each monad is a permanent substratum that loses old properties and acquires new ones.

Whitehead is unsatisfied with this Aristotelian account of the monads' ontological structure for several reasons. How is it possible to conceive of *energetic* monads in terms of the *static* notion of an underlying bearer? The notion of substance as a substratum clashes with Leibniz's other fundamental idea that a substance is *essentially* a being capable of action. And how could categories such as 'thing' and 'properties' be of any use in describing ultimate principles? These categories were developed by primitive men in primitive times to deal with ordinary material objects such as, for example, heavy rocks, fallen trees and impervious mountains. These concepts are of great practical utility, but they were not meant to have any deep ontological significance; our ancestors worried about their bare animal survival, not about subtle metaphysical questions.

But the main obstacle that prevents understanding monads as substrata, Whitehead argues, is their experiential nature. The concept of the monad as embodying a point of view is a thoroughly relational concept. We *experience* the world by grasping and incorporating aspects of it into the unity of a new perspective. This process must involve, for Whitehead, some sort of actual relationship between the experiencing subject and the experienced object. But there is no place for relations within a metaphysical scheme that acknowledges only the reality of properties and their underlying bearers.

As noted in the previous chapter, within such a scheme reality collapses into a plurality of mutually isolated substances:

> The doctrine of the individual independence of real facts is derived from the notion that the subject–predicate form of statement conveys a truth which is metaphysically ultimate. (PR 137)

In Whitehead's view, Leibniz has grasped the truth about the ultimate constituents of reality, but lacks the conceptuality with which to express it. Worse than this, the concepts he eventually adopts – the notions of a substratum and its properties – embody a metaphysical point of view that is the exact opposite of the one he wishes to express. These Aristotelian notions privilege permanence over flux, inertness over activity, mutual separateness over relatedness. Only with the 'deposition of substance-quality' ontology, he contends, can we 'reject the notion of individual substances, each with its private world of qualities and sensations' (PR 160).

According to Whitehead, it was precisely in order to soften this tension at the heart of his metaphysics that Leibniz developed the doctrine of pre-established harmony, according to which the monads' perceptions have been synchronised by God. This theory enables Leibniz to hold that monads are experientially connected, while at the same time denying that they are causally related:

> [Leibniz] had . . . on his hands two distinct points of view. One was that the final real entity is an organizing activity, fusing ingredients into a unity, so that this unity is the reality. The other point of view is that the final real entities are substances supporting qualities. The first point of view depends upon the acceptance of internal relations binding together all reality. The latter is inconsistent with the reality of such relations. To combine these two points of view, his monads were therefore windowless; and their passions merely mirrored the universe by the divine arrangement of a pre-established harmony. (SMW 155)

In Whitehead's eyes, the theory of pre-established harmony is an artificial device the only purpose of which is to conceal the inner tension that pervades Leibniz's system.

WHITEHEAD AND LEIBNIZ ON THE NATURE OF CAUSATION

In *Modes of Thought*, Whitehead remarks:

> The mere notion of transferring a quality is entirely unintelligible. Suppose that two occurrences may be in fact detached so that one

of them is comprehensible without reference to the other. Then all notion of causation between them, or conditioning, becomes unintelligible. (MT 164)

This is an allusion to that crucial passage in the *Monadology* in which Leibniz explains why monads cannot be affected from without:

> The monads have no windows through which something can enter or leave. Accidents cannot be detached, nor can they go about outside of substances, as the sensible species of the Scholastics once did. Thus, neither substance nor accident can enter a monad from without. (AG 214, §7)

The passage may be read as providing some evidence in support of the thesis that monads are, for Leibniz, bearers of properties, as well as that there is a close connection between this Aristotelian conception and the denial of direct causal interaction. Leibniz is here namely concerned with that type of causal fact in which a substance A acts upon an already existing substance B, so as to produce an alteration in B. Leibniz denies that monads can be related in this way by means of the following argument:

1. Causation (in the sense of a substance's ability to produce an alteration in another substance's state) involves the transference of some one element from one substance A to another substance B.
2. On an Aristotelian substance-predicate ontology, the transferred element must be either the active substance or one of its properties.
3. Substances cannot become parts of other substances; for substances are simple, not complex. Hence, the transferred element will have to be a property.
4. During the transaction from substance A to substance B, there will be a moment in which the transferred property does not belong to either A or B. This is inconceivable, since properties require a *substratum* in which to inhere.
5. Hence, on an Aristotelian substance-predicate ontology, direct causal interaction between monads is impossible, as neither substances nor properties can be exchanged.

To someone convinced that causal relations are real, this reasoning will look like a further argument against the thesis (involved with premise (2)) that substances are substrata, which is precisely how Whitehead reads it. What is noteworthy is that Whitehead doesn't interpret this argument, as he would be entitled to do from a logical point of view, as a *reductio* of premise (1) – the influx model of causation that Leibniz derives from the late Scholastics. As a matter of fact – and against Hume's contention that causation can be understood only as correlation – Whitehead shares with Leibniz the notion that causation involves some kind of flowing in, a transference of elements from the causally active substance to the affected one. Trying to explain his rejection of direct monadic interaction to De Volder, Leibniz says: 'Properly speaking, I don't admit the action of substances on one another, since there appears to be no way for one monad to flow into another' (AG 176).

The challenge of providing an alternative to the theory of pre-established harmony thus becomes, for Whitehead, the question of how to make sense of monadic influx in categories different from those of substance and property.

INTERACTING MONADS: INTRODUCING THE CONCEPT OF *PREHENSION*

What remains of the monad once the concept of substratum has been rejected? Radically new ontological categories are needed and one main way to discover them is by examining the monad as this is concretely given. This is possible in Whitehead's philosophy because the subject of experience is here posited as one of the models for metaphysical generalisation. Our own inner life shows, in other words, what the fundamental constituents of reality are like. As we have seen, Whitehead thinks that Descartes had a glimpse of this methodological truth, but failed to realise its full metaphysical significance. Whitehead makes its relevance fully explicit in what he terms the reformed subjectivist principle, this being the notion 'that the whole universe consists of elements disclosed in the analysis of the experiences of subjects' (PR 166).

What does such an analysis reveal? In consonance with James's account of the self in *The Principles of Psychology* (cf. SMW 143ff.),

Whitehead contends that our conscious life comes as a series of 'pulses' or 'throbs' of experience.³ The stream of consciousness is broken into a plurality of successive quanta of feeling, each of which lasts for a brief period of time. Such total moments of experience Whitehead calls 'actual occasions' (or, alternatively, 'actual entities'), and he offers them as substitutes for Leibniz's monads (cf. AI 177). The new ontology Whitehead settles for is one of serially interconnected experiential events:

> The soul is nothing else than the succession of my occasions of experience, extending from birth to the present moment. (MT 163)

Each occasion of experience must be conceived as possessing *duration*. As an experience such as the hearing of a melody wonderfully illustrates, an experience requires a timespan in which to unfold. Whitehead appeals to James's analyses in *Some Problems of Philosophy* (1910) to substantiate this claim:

> Either your experience is of no content, of no change, or it is of a perceptible amount of content or change. Your acquaintance with reality grows literally by buds or drops of perception. Intellectually and on reflection you can divide these into components, but as immediately given, they come totally or not at all. (James, as quoted in PR 68)

How are such successive occasions related? Consider our experiences when we are sitting in a silent room and thunder suddenly breaks in. What we experience then is not merely the sound of the thunder, but the *breaking* of the previous silence through it. As James noticed in *The Principles of Psychology*, this would not be possible if the silence of a moment ago were not still included within the novel moment in which the breaking of the thunder is experienced:

> Into the awareness of the thunder itself the awareness of the previous silence creeps and continues; for what we hear when the thunder crashes is not thunder *pure*, but thunder-breaking-upon-silence-and-contrasting-with-it. Our feeling of the same objective thunder, coming in this way, is quite different from

what it would be were the thunder a continuation of previous
thunder. The thunder itself we believe to abolish and exclude
the silence; but the *feeling* of the thunder is also a feeling of the
silence as just gone. (PP 241)

Or consider our hearing of a musical melody. We couldn't experience any music as a flowing piece if the notes just past were not also included in our present awareness. These examples show that there is a kind of natural 'fusing' within our conscious stream of its successive experiential occasions. As James put it, our successive states of consciousness 'melt into each other like dissolving views' (PP 248).

The kind of phenomenon James is drawing our attention to here is the one Husserl calls *retention*, an apt term that will be used in what follows. Whitehead goes beyond Husserl and James in that he provides a metaphysical as opposed to a merely phenomenological account of this phenomenon. Retention is for him the way in which an immediately past occasion of experience leaves a mark upon – and thereby conditions – a novel moment of experience. In other words, Whitehead suggests, we should interpret retention as a form of mental causation – as an 'influx' of aspects of the past moment of experience within the novel one.

In order to understand Whitehead's view correctly it is important to realise that the term 'influx' is not used by him in a metaphorical sense. The elements retained in the novel occasion are actual components of the previous occasion of mentality, not mere *representation*s of them. Whitehead coined the term 'prehension' to designate this incorporation of aspects of past experiences. The concept is introduced by way of a comparison with Leibniz:

[Leibniz] employed the terms 'perception' and 'apperception'
for the lower and higher ways in which one monad can take
account of another, namely for ways of awareness. But these
terms . . . *are all entangled in the notion of representative
perception which I reject* . . . Accordingly, on the Leibnizian
model, I use the term 'prehension' for the general way in which
the occasion of experience can include, as part of its own
essence, any other entity. (AI 234; my emphasis)

This is an intricate passage. In the first place, Whitehead emphasises that retained contents are not duplicates (*representative perceptions*) of previous experiences, but the original experiences themselves. How can this be on the pulse-model of the self? Are past pulses not simply dead and gone? Whitehead denies this to be the case; past experiences, or more precisely, aspects of them, *genuinely prolong their life* by being incorporated into later occasions. (This is a crucial point, which will be considered more carefully at the end of this section.)

Secondly, Whitehead explains that the relation between two successive occasions within our stream of consciousness has a double nature. Viewed from the standpoint of the past occasion, the experiential influx involved in the phenomenon of retention is a basic form of causation. Viewed from the perspective of the novel occasion, that influx is to be regarded as an elementary, unconscious form of perception. Let A, B and C be three occasions in the causal past of the present occasion of experience M. Then it is true to say that

> the (unconscious) direct perception of A, B and C is merely the causal efficacy of A, B, and C as elements in the constitution of M. Such direct perception will suffer from vagueness . . . There may thus remain a sense of the causal efficacy of actual presences, whose exact relationships in the external world are shrouded. (PR 116)

This account of causation goes to the very heart of Whitehead's critique of Leibniz: Whitehead is putting together again in his concept of prehension what Leibniz wants to keep distinct with his theory of pre-established harmony – the capacity to perceive on the one hand, that of being directly acted upon on the other. (Indeed, even if causally insulated, Leibniz's monads are not solitary Cartesian selves, but genuine 'perceivers' of an externally existing world. Monads are so little to be equated with solipsistic minds that the *epistemological* notion of clarity of perception even becomes a criterion for establishing an *ontological* hierarchy: higher monads 'more truly' *know* what the world looks like.)[4]

Thirdly, Whitehead draws a comparison with Leibniz's concept of 'perception'. This is a way of emphasising the fact that the type of experience he calls 'prehension' is a primitive, low-level one; it can, yet need not, be made the object of a higher order thought or experience (Leibniz's 'apperception').

As already hinted above, Whitehead's account of causation in terms of the double notion of influx/prehension is a startling one. One first major problem is that the kind of mental determination envisaged by Whitehead seems insufficient to account for causal relations between occasions pertaining to other individuals' experiential streams. Whitehead argues, on the contrary, that his account can be generalised to *all* existing occasions. Stated in Scholastic terminology, there is no fundamental distinction between 'immanent' and 'transeunt' causation – that is to say, between causation that remains within the agent (conceived as a series of momentary mental occurrences) and causation between different agents. The principles I discover in myself have universal validity:

> in so far as we apply notions of causation to the understanding of events in nature, we must conceive these events under the general notions which apply to occasions of experience. For we can only understand causation in terms of our observations of these occasions. (AI 184)

This is a crucial, yet highly theoretically laden passage. One way to put mind back into nature, Whitehead assumes, is by conceiving of an occasion of human mentality as being itself a natural event. How this is precisely to be understood will be considered in the next chapter. For the time being, the point to be noticed is that this belief enables Whitehead to argue that, by inspecting our own subjectivity, we are also inspecting nature. A conception of causation constructed on the basis of an examination of our own self can therefore be legitimately (which does not mean infallibly) interpreted as providing an insight into the nature of physical causation. If one recognises that mind is a fully natural event, in other words, one does not have to acquiesce in the sceptical belief that the very being of causation, conceived not as mere regularity but as a real link between physical events, is bound to remain forever beyond our knowledge.

On this generalised theory of causation, however, there is no reason in principle why a person should not be able to retain elements *from the minds of other persons*, which sounds indeed a little implausible. Not everyone will agree with this sceptical evaluation. The fact that Whitehead's theory accounts for the possibility of an interchange between occasions constituting different personal streams may be viewed by some as a promising matrix for understanding parapsychological phenomena or religious experiences.[5] Whitehead seems willing to admit telepathy as a real phenomenon (cf. PR 308). And at one point he denies that knowledge of other minds is possible only by way of interpretation of our immediate sensory perceptions: 'The claim that the cognition of alien mentalities must necessarily be by means of indirect inferences from aspects of shape and of sense-objects is wholly unwarranted by the philosophy of organism' (SMW 150). All this is difficult to refute, but it does strain credulity.

Another objection to Whitehead's account is that it seems faulty even as an explanation of immanent causation, a point that was already hinted at above. Whitehead clarifies the nature of the causal link thus:

> All relatedness [between occasions] . . . is wholly concerned
> with the appropriation of the dead by the living – that is to say,
> with 'objective immortality' whereby what is divested of its
> own living immediacy becomes a real component in other living
> immediacies of becoming. (PR xiii–xiv)

As a way of illustration, consider the previous example of our hearing a piece of music. When we hear a melody, the notes just heard keep resonating in the present moment, yet they have lost their character of *presentness* (their 'living immediacy') and have acquired a character of *pastness* ('objective immortality'). The notes are apprehended as belonging to the past – as feeble versions or echoes of the originals. This is correct from a purely phenomenological point of view, yet Whitehead also provides a metaphysical interpretation of the phenomenon of retention as involving a real entrance of the past into the present. But how could the retained experience and the experience originally felt be numerically the same, if they come with a different qualitative feel? This is impossible. One cannot divorce the appearance of an experience from what that experience is in the way required by Whitehead's account; an experience, considered as such, simply *is* what it feels like.[6] (This is, incidentally, a lesson Whitehead apparently failed to learn from William James, who in *The Principles of Psychology* writes: 'the essence of feeling is to be felt, and as a psychic existent *feels*, so it must *be*' (PP 163).)

Based on this account, Whitehead's attempt to install windows in Leibniz's monads can hardly be regarded as successful. Whitehead's theory of actual occasions, however, is more complex – and surprising – than it may appear at first sight.

NOTES

1. John Locke, *An Essay Concerning Human Understanding* (1689), ed. Peter H. Nidditch, Oxford: Oxford University Press, 1975, II.XXIII.1.
2. Ibid., II.XIII.10.
3. Galen Strawson advocates a theory of this kind in *Selves: An Essay in Revisionary Metaphysics*, Oxford: Clarendon Press, 2009; for an earlier and much briefer version of his argument, see his 'The Self and the Sesmet', *Journal of Consciousness Studies* 6/4, 1999, pp. 99–135. What may be called 'pulse-theories of the self' are also discussed by T. L. S. Sprigge in *James and Bradley: American Truth and British Reality*, Chicago: Open Court, 1993, pp. 84–97 (with respect to James) and pp. 522–32 (with respect to Bradley). The term 'pulse' is used by James in his *Principles of Psychology* in the context of a discussion of the problem of the unity of consciousness: 'Whatever things are thought in relation are thought from the outset in a unity, in a *single pulse of subjectivity*, a single psychosis, feeling, or state of mind' (PP 278; my emphasis).
4. Not all monads are worthy of being called 'souls', but only those 'where perception is more distinct and accompanied by memory' (AG 215, §19). An even higher grade of reality is achieved by those monads that are endowed with self-awareness and knowledge of God (AG 217, §29).
5. This view is advocated by David Ray Griffin in his remarkable *Unsnarling the World-Knot: Consciousness, Freedom and the Mind–Body Problem*, Berkeley: University of California Press, 1998, pp. 206–7.

6. For an objection along these lines, see T. L. S. Sprigge, *The Vindication of Absolute Idealism*, Edinburgh: Edinburgh University Press, 1983, p. 230, and P. Basile, *Leibniz, Whitehead and the Metaphysics of Causation*, Basingstoke and New York: Palgrave Macmillan, 2009, pp. 100–4.

CHAPTER 5

Overcoming the Cartesian Legacy: The Process Concept of Substance

THE ACTUAL OCCASION AS A SUBJECT-SUPERJECT

It was argued in Chapter 1 that Whitehead rejects both materialism and traditional metaphysical idealism. What he strives to develop is a radically novel conception of the basic constituents of reality, one capable of bridging the gap between the 'mental' and the 'physical' without sacrificing either of these two apparently heterogeneous poles by declaring one of them unreal. Now it is time to turn to a direct consideration of this issue; this requires discussing some further aspects of Whitehead's complex notion of an actual occasion.

A moment of human mentality involves more than the retention of past experiences. Imagine you are reading a book in your room when you hear someone walking along the street. The steps suddenly enter your conscious awareness, while many of the pleasant phantasies and sensations associated with the reading vanish. Some elements have been retained, others have been excluded. At the same time, you experience the steps as an evolving series. They seem to be arising from the past, but there is also a suggestion in your present consciousness that they will continue into the immediate future. Each moment of experience is a Janus-faced entity. It has a selective relationship with things just gone, while also foreshadowing events to come: 'The present,' Whitehead writes, 'bears in its own realized constitution relationships to a future beyond itself' (AI 191).[1] As he alternatively puts it: '[e]ach moment of experience confesses itself to be a transition between two worlds, the immediate past and the immediate future' (AI 192).

This phenomenological analysis provides the basis for the metaphysical doctrine that each experiential occasion begins its life as a *subject* that incorporates aspects of its precursor, before suffering deposition by turning into an *object* for a new occasion. In retrospect, an individual's psychical life is a chain of moments of experience that have become available for prehensions to later actualities. Whitehead's actual occasions are *subjects-becoming-objects*: 'The occasion arises from relevant objects, and perishes into the status of an object for other occasions' (AI 177). As Whitehead explains, it has been the mistake of philosophical tradition to think that 'subject' and 'object' were synonymous of 'knower' and 'known'. This is a very one-sided interpretation of these concepts. The term 'knower' suggests conscious discrimination, which is a high form of mentality; obviously enough, however, knowledge in the full sense of the term cannot be ascribed to all actualities in nature.

Undoubtedly, this metaphysical theory has some grounding in our phenomenology. But a question immediately arises: how does a novel actual occasion come into being? Whitehead's answer – the doctrine of *concrescence* – is one of the most puzzling of his entire metaphysics. Since we entertain genuine causal relationships with many things in our environment, each occasion must incorporate within itself (prehend) aspects of myriad other occasions, that is to say, not just of the occasions belonging to its personal history, but also of occasions entering into the constitution of other physical entities. As Whitehead also notices, there is no non-arbitrary way to sharply distinguish between those regions of the world that constitute our environment and those that do not; strictly speaking, the entire cosmos can be said to be our environment. Not all aspects of the external world, however, can possibly be absorbed within one single moment of experience. These simple reflections suggest that a mental occasion must be the outcome of a genetic process that involves *selection* of causal influences as well as their *integration* into an ordered whole. Once again, Whitehead remarks, Leibniz had some grasp of the truth when he said that each monad embodies a 'perspective' upon the entire universe.

'Concrescence' (a term chosen for its etymological suggestiveness, since it means 'growing together') is Whitehead's name for an actual occasion's genetic process. Its analysis forces him to refine considerably his notion of 'prehension' as 'the general way in which the occasion of experience can include, as part of its own essence, any other entity' (AI 234). The most salient aspects of Whitehead's understanding of this genetic process can be briefly tabulated as follows.

In the first place, Whitehead observes, some experienced contents must be prevented from entering into the final occasion of experience. This leads to a distinction between 'positive' and 'negative' prehensions:

> An actual entity has a perfectly definite bond with each item in the universe. This determinate bond is its prehension of that item. A negative prehension is the definite exclusion of that item from positive contribution to the subject's own real internal constitution. This doctrine involves the position that a negative prehension expresses a bond. A positive prehension is the definite inclusion of that item into positive contribution to the subject's own real internal constitution. (PR 41)

Why does Whitehead say that a negative prehension 'expresses a bond', rather than the lack of one, given that its function is to prevent a datum from entering into the constitution of the novel occasion? There is, even in ordinary speech, an obvious difference between *ignoring (not being aware of something)* and *excluding (intentionally preventing something from participation)*. The exclusion of past actualities is made in the interest of realising a unified result, a definite moment of experience. The excluded contents are therefore not simply *ignored* by the emergent actuality, but are positively *taken notice of* (which justifies using the term 'prehension' at all). In some mysterious way, such contents are 'evaluated' by the emergent occasion, which 'judges' that their incorporation would hinder, rather than promote, the creation of a unified moment of experience.[2]

Secondly, the contents admitted for inclusion must issue in a determinate result, the 'final' or 'satisfied' occasion. This means that they must be synthesised and ordered. Accordingly, Whitehead draws a further distinction between 'physical' and 'mental' (or 'conceptual') prehensions: while the former refers to an occasion's ability to incorporate aspects of other occasions (the 'influx' discussed in the previous chapter), the latter stands for an occasion's capacity to envision *abstract forms*. Awareness of forms must be postulated, for otherwise the concrescence, which is a teleological process aiming at a definite result, a wholly determinate quantum of mentality, would lack any directive principle: 'A conceptual prehension is a direct vision . . . of some possibility as to how actualities *may* be *definite*' (PR 33). The form of definiteness that constitutes the end that the concrescence strives to actualise is said to be the concrescence's 'subjective aim'.

Thirdly, Whitehead emphasises that the process of concrescence is not a deterministic one. It is a genuinely creative process in which the outcome is indeed conditioned, yet not wholly prescribed, by the causal data available to the concrescing occasion. In what sounds like a questionable appeal to traditional terminology, Whitehead contends that it is in this sense, and only in this sense, that a substance can be said to be *causa sui*. As he puts it: 'To be *causa sui* means that the process of concrescence is its own reason for the decision in respect to the qualitative clothing of feelings' (PR 88). We do all have a sense of being free agents in a larger world; the concrescence is *the* 'locus' where our own metaphysical spontaneity expresses itself.

Finally, since the occasion of mentality that constitutes a person's mind at any one moment is the outcome of a synthetic process, the question arises as to the nature of the agent that is in charge of it. *Who or what is doing the synthesis?* This question is a particularly perplexing one. Since the momentary occasion of experience is the outcome of the concrescing process, no self has yet emerged to be charged with this responsibility. Whitehead does not hesitate to draw the only possible conclusion open to him. There is literally nothing to the genetic process other than the process itself – the process *is* the becoming, emerging self. The point is illustrated thus:

> The philosophies of substance presuppose a subject which then encounters a datum, and then reacts to the datum. The philosophy of organism presupposes a datum which is met with feelings, and progressively attains the unity of a subject. (PR 155)

The 'datum' in question is represented by the actualities just gone. They have already achieved the ecstatic peak of satisfaction and are now available to the emerging actualities as 'objects' or 'materials' for their own self-creation. '[T]he actualities,' Whitehead writes, 'are moments of passage into a new stage of publicity . . . Prehensions have public careers, but they are born privately' (PR 290).

Insofar as it is considered as the outcome of the concrescing process, Whitehead remarks, what is usually termed 'subject' should be called 'superject'. The actual occasion – whose full nature consists of both process and outcome – is therefore best characterised as *subject-superject*. In his discussion of the nature of the self, Whitehead praises Kant for having 'fully and explicitly, introduced into philosophy the conception of an act of experience as a constructive functioning' (PR 156). He arguably overestimates the similarity between his own theory and Kant's, however. The Kantian notion of the experienced world as constructed by the subject on the basis of a manifold of empirical data is indeed revolutionary, but it is not as radically revisionary of our ordinary modes of thought as Whitehead's. However one tries, it is difficult not to think of Kant's Transcendental Ego as a kind of underlying receptacle for empirical data, a Humean theatre 'where several perceptions successively make their appearance; pass, re-pass, glide away, and mingle in an infinite variety of postures and situations'.[3] Kant's concept of 'synthesis', it should also be remembered, is an epistemological, not a metaphysical one.

At one point in *Process and Reality*, Whitehead nicely summarises his view as follows:

> It is fundamental to the metaphysical doctrine of the philosophy of organism, that the notion of an actual entity as the unchanging subject of change is completely abandoned. An actual entity is at once the subject experiencing and the superject of its experiences. It is subject-superject, and neither half of the description can for a moment be lost sight of.
> (PR 29)

This is a surprising conception. If Whitehead is right in claiming that Aristotelian ontology shapes our thoughts as well as our modes of expression, however, then this is precisely the sort of idea that – at the present stage of metaphysical inquiry – we should find it difficult to grasp as well as to articulate clearly.

THE ACTUAL OCCASION AS A SPACE-TIME QUANTUM

This account of the actual occasion as a subject-superject is puzzling enough. Can it be reconciled with Whitehead's other fundamental claim, namely that actual occasions are the constituents of the physical world? The problem is that the notion of a subject-superject would seem to involve a form of metaphysical idealism (or, as it should perhaps be better called, 'mentalism'), according to which reality's building blocks are mind-like entities. Some passages would seem to support this mentalistic interpretation; for example, Whitehead argues at one point that with the introduction of the notion of prehension/objectification 'the way is . . . opened for a rational scheme of cosmology in which a final reality is identified with acts of experience' (PR 143). The *esse* of reality may not be *percipi*, Whitehead would seem here to be arguing, but it certainly is *percipere*. If an actual occasion is nothing but a moment of experience, however, it becomes somewhat difficult to see how material objects could turn out to possess more than a phenomenal status, as Leibniz observed in the short note he wrote in his copy of Berkeley's *Treatise*.

This would be too hasty a conclusion to draw. Whitehead's concept of experience (and of the way it fits into the physical world) needs further discussion before the radical novelty of the concept of an actual occasion can be properly appreciated.

As a matter of fact, the characterisation of the actual entity as a subject-superject is not the sole one that Whitehead provides in *Process and Reality*. As explained in Chapter 1, in *Science and the Modern World* he had rejected the Newtonian view of time and space as the two great containers of all things. As an alternative, he now introduces the notion that actual occasions are inherently spatio-temporal events. While coming into being, they cumulate to form an intricate spatio-temporal block, an ever-growing manifold of interrelated occasions. The events are not *in* time or *in* space, they *constitute* space-time. Whitehead means it literally when he says:

> The actualities of the Universe are processes of experience, each process an individual fact. The whole Universe is the advancing assemblage of these processes. (AI 197)

You can imagine the universe expanding like a drop of ink on a piece of paper; except that there is no paper on which to expand.

To be precise, Whitehead does not speak of space-time in *Process and Reality*, but of an *extensive continuum*. What we ordinarily refer to as space and time is an abstract scheme of relationships of the highest generality that can exist only on the basis of the concrete whole constituted by the actual occasions. This notion contrasts with our ordinary Newtonian conceptions. The temptation to understand the extensive continuum as an encompassing dimension after the fashion of common sense should nevertheless be carefully resisted. The extensive continuum, Whitehead says, is a 'specialized ordering of the concrete occasions and of the prehensions into which they are divisible' (PR 293).

Since Whitehead also writes that the 'extensive continuum is one relational complex in which all potential objectifications find their niche' (PR 66), it is tempting to think of it as a pre-existing plenum of sorts – that is to say, as an underlying Reality of a quasi-Spinozian kind that is constantly filled with new emerging occasions. In an important passage, however, Whitehead carefully explains how his system differs from Spinoza's:

> The philosophy of organism is closely allied to Spinoza's scheme of thought. But it differs by the abandonment of the subject–predicate forms of thought, so far as concerns the presupposition that this form is a direct embodiment of the most ultimate characterization of fact. The result is that the 'substance-quality' concept is avoided; and that morphological description is replaced by description of dynamic process. Also Spinoza's 'modes' now become the sheer actualities; so that, though analysis of them increases our understanding, it does not lead us to the discovery of any higher grade of reality. (PR 7)

First, and as the context in which the passage is embedded makes clear, Spinoza is praised for having renounced Cartesian dualism; this is why the philosophy of organism is allied to 'Spinoza's scheme of thought'. Secondly, Whitehead makes the by now well-known point that reality cannot be understood in terms of the Aristotelian categories of subject and predicate. Thirdly, he says that, with the deposition of that ontological paradigm, Spinoza's 'modes' (the particular entities in nature) have to be reconceptualised as 'actual occasions'. Lastly, he emphasises that there is no higher Reality over and above the occasions in his system. In sum – and as he repeatedly contends in many passages of *Process and Reality* – 'the ultimate metaphysical truth is atomism' (PR 35; cf. PR 18). Admittedly, the word 'atomism' is highly misleading, probably even ill chosen, not just because of its strong materialistic connotations, but because atoms are traditionally conceived as being mutually independent. Whitehead's actual occasions, on the contrary, are existentially connected by virtue of their prehensive bonds. What Whitehead wants to convey by the term is just the fact that reality is constituted 'bottom-up' rather than, as in monistic systems like Spinoza's, 'top-down'.

This forceful rejection of Spinoza's metaphysics makes it at any rate clear that space and time cannot have any independent reality apart from the concrete web of particular actual occasions. The reason why Whitehead argues that each developing occasion eventually occupies a place within the extensive continuum is simply that a specific system of spatio-temporal relations is already in place when a new occasion comes into being. This system is not 'pre-existent' in an absolute sense, but solely relative to each novel occasion.

The longer passage just quoted in which Whitehead briefly summarises the differences between his own philosophy of organism and Spinoza's substance monism does, however, also generate a problem. In Spinoza's system, the heterogeneity of mind (thought) and matter (extension) is fully acknowledged. Mind and matter are not fully divorced, however, since they are conceived as parallel (not causally interacting) manifestations of a single Substance. In this way, Spinoza thinks, his system can account for the connection between the mental and the physical without renouncing the idea that they are different in nature. Mind and matter are distinct from one another, yet they are linked by the common Substance that they express.

This beautifully simple explanation is not available to Whitehead any more. With his rejection of the concept of an underlying (or, as it should perhaps be better put, an 'all-encompassing') Substance, the problem of modelling the relation between the physical and the mental opens up again. The two dimensions must now either be wholly detached from one another or collapse into one. The former path yields the Cartesian bifurcation of nature that Whitehead abhors; the latter is precisely the result he is aiming at. But how can actual occasions have material (spatio-temporal) properties, if they are subjects of experience?

This is the crucial juncture at which some readers may find it difficult, perhaps even impossible, to accept the conclusion of Whitehead's chain of reasoning. On the face of it, one may want to object, we are left with two incompatible characterisations of the actual occasion:

1. The actual occasion is a quantum of experience: 'each actual entity is a throb of experience including the actual world within its scope' (PR 190).
2. The actual occasion is a spatio-temporal quantum: 'There is a spatial element in the quantum as well as a temporal element' (PR 283).

Can the appearance of inconsistency be dispelled?

For the sake of analysis, the temporal and the spatial aspects of the actual occasion may be considered separately. It could be thought that there is no special problem in conceiving of an occasion as temporal, since each drop of experience possesses internal duration. But Whitehead also identifies 'physical time' with the successive series of durational wholes. This relegates the process of concrescence, mysteriously, to a pre-temporal or non-temporal realm of existence. 'The actual entity,' Whitehead says, 'is the enjoyment of a certain quantum of physical time. But the genetic process [the concrescence] is not the temporal succession' (PR 283). 'This genetic passage from phase to phase,' he also adds, 'is not in physical time' (PR 283). And even more puzzlingly, he writes:

> in every act of becoming [the concrescence] there is the becoming of something with temporal extension [the realised occasion]; but . . . the act itself is not extensive, in the sense that it is divisible into earlier and later acts of becoming which correspond to the extensive divisibility of what has become. (PR 69)

Several problems arise at once. How can a process, such as the concrescence is said to be, fail to have a temporal dimension? How can what is not temporal, the concrescence, bring about a temporal product, the subjectively enjoyed duration? Or is Whitehead only talking metaphorically when he describes the concrescence as a process that develops in successive phases? These questions find no easy answer in Whitehead's metaphysics.[4]

Analogously, it could be argued that there is an obvious sense in which our mind can be said to be spatial, since we do have perceptions of voluminous things located in space. In describing actual occasions as spatial quanta, however, Whitehead is conceiving of them as *constituents of real space*, not simply as having internal spatial representations. This means that actual occasions have to be thought of as being themselves voluminous. This *must* be so, it should be noted, if the natural world, of which the actual occasions are the basic building blocks, has to be more than a phenomenal appearance. But conceived as a quantum of experience (that is, as subject-superject), the occasion can hardly be subsumed under spatial categories. Or is it rather that our ordinary conceptions of space and experience are both radically defective? Leibniz's monads, having no parts, have 'neither extension, nor shape' (AG 213, §3). Do Whitehead's voluminous actual occasions have each its own distinct shape? Whitehead does not say, yet they must have if they are not solely temporally, but also spatially, extended.

Alternatively, one may try to make the two descriptions (1) and (2) consistent by taking them to refer to successive phases of an actual occasion's career. The occasion would then begin its life as a causally open process (the concrescence); evolve creatively into a unified moment of experience (the superject); and eventually turn into a constituent of the physical world. Such a suggestion makes the contrast between (1) and (2) less strident. But again, does it work as a philosophical theory? That an *experiential process* should issue in a *spatial quantum* is as magical a leap as the alleged origination of mind from merely extended matter discussed in Chapter 1. On a conventional understanding of space, what was there called 'the heterogeneity problem' arises again – only now in reverse order.

That the problem of unifying different descriptions of the same entity would at some stage emerge in Whitehead's philosophy was only to be expected, since as explained in Chapter 3 his notions are achieved as generalisations from different starting points. Moreover, the notion of an actual occasion is precisely one of those ultimate generalities that can be understood – and articulated linguistically – only when metaphysical knowledge has achieved full completion. To the best of my knowledge, nowhere does Whitehead suggest that he has made anything more than a first, tentative start at metaphysical generalisation.

THE LANGUAGE OF EXPERIENCE: INSIGHT OR DELUSION?

The conclusion of the previous examination can now be summarised as follows. Whitehead's substances are spatial-temporal-experiential event-units. If one associates the spatial and temporal dimension of an occasion with the concept of the 'physical', the experiential with the concept of the 'psychical', then actual occasions can be said to be 'psycho-physical' events. This is the conception Whitehead was aiming at in *Science and the Modern World*. In spite of his characterisation of actual occasions as occasions of experience, he is not advocating a traditional form of metaphysical idealism (or mentalism) but a form of panpsychism or, as it is also sometimes called, 'panexperientialism'.[5]

Because of its radical novelty, however, Whitehead's view is easy to misunderstand. The point is worth repeating: he is not simply arguing that the basic building blocks of reality have a 'physical' as well as a 'mental' *component*, which would be dualism in disguise. The proposed view is that, at a fundamental level of analysis, *experience* is *physical* reality. The 'mental' and the 'physical' are, literally, one and the same. Whitehead could not be clearer as to this:

> An occasion of experience which includes a human mentality is an extreme instance . . . of those happenings which constitute nature. (AI 184)

This does not imply, of course, that all actual occasions have the rich experiences characteristic of a human being, which is why human mentality is said to be an '*extreme* instance' of natural happenings, instead of merely an instance. Which components of our experience can be regarded as distinctively human is, of course, open for discussion. But it is clear that the universal experiential features will have to be the more primitive ones. Addressing this question, Whitehead notes: 'the emotional appetitive elements in our conscious experience are those which most closely resemble the basic elements of all *physical experience*' (PR 163; my emphasis). Interestingly, Whitehead uses here the expression 'physical experience'. His view would indeed be better called 'physicalist panexperientialism' (or, alternatively, 'panexperientialist physicalism'), rather than 'panpsychism' or 'panexperientialism' *tout court*.

Understanding Whitehead's notion of a 'physical experience' is not easy, since it involves a drastic revision of ordinary conceptions of 'experience', 'space' and 'time.' Is Whitehead's view genuinely intelligible? Sceptical worries could perhaps be articulated thus: if Whitehead really wanted to overcome the mind–body dualism, why did he retain such terms as 'experience', 'mind', 'subject' and the like? Aren't the objections raised in the previous section against the notion of an actual occasion as an experiential/physical unit due to the fact that we are still thinking within the inhibiting framework set by Cartesian metaphysics and forms of expression? If so, as Whitehead would surely contend, why not simply get rid of all this philosophically loaded, inadequate language?

In the end, Whitehead suggests, this is exactly what we should have to do. Consider, for example, what he says in *Process and Reality* about his use of the word 'feeling':

> This word 'feeling' is a mere technical term; but it has been chosen to suggest that functioning through which the concrescent actuality appropriates its datum so as to make it its own. (PR 164)

This is a striking passage. To say that a word has a technical sense is to say that it diverges in some important respect from its ordinary usage. But how significant is this divergence, according to Whitehead? As he makes clear in the above passage, the word 'feeling' is used in *Process and Reality* in a *twisted* sense. He is obliged to speak in terms of the traditional philosophical vocabulary, simply because there is no other from which to start, but words are now used elliptically to convey new, as yet unexpressed meanings.

This is a particularly important instance of the general problem that language poses to the revisionary metaphysician that was discussed at the very beginning of this book. Has Whitehead managed to solve it successfully? Do we understand what he means when he says that an occasion 'feels' other actualities, granted that 'feeling' (and by implication, words such as 'experience', 'self', 'emotion') does not carry the familiar signification? We sense that language is stretched to its breaking point when encountering a passage such as the following:

The final facts are, all alike, actual entities; and these actual entities are drops of experience, complex and interdependent. (PR 18)

Eventually, each reader is called upon to decide whether she or he understands what Whitehead – here and in many other analogous places – *means* to convey. Is he opening a new conceptual horizon, or is he simply talking nonsense? It lies in the nature of the case that there will be no non-controversial answer to this, all-decisive, question.

SUBSTANCE REVISITED: A LOOK AHEAD

Before bringing this chapter to an end, it is important to appreciate how Whitehead's reconstruction of the conception of substance also involves a drastic revision of traditional ontological ways of thinking. His rejection of the cluster of notions most closely associated with the logical conception of substance as a subject of predication (items 3–5) was discussed in Chapter 4. What remains to be considered is how the concept of prehension involves a rejection of the other dimensions (items 6–8) of the traditional concept. Three points are particularly worth making:

1. Whitehead's substances are occasions of experience that absorb aspects of other actualities. As such, they are literally *constituted* by other occasions. Contrary to the traditional understanding, actual entities are *not* ontologically independent. As Whitehead puts it: 'no individual subject can have independent reality, since it is a prehension of limited aspects of subjects other than itself' (SMW 151).
2. The notion that no substance can in any sense be a part of another substance is presupposed as obvious in premise (3) of Leibniz's argument against causal interaction, considered in Chapter 3. But in Whitehead's theory, prehended occasions are real constituents of other occasions. A substance *can* therefore be part of another substance. This new account of substance, Whitehead points out, 'directly traverses Aristotle's dictum, "A substance is not present in a subject." On the contrary ... an actual entity *is* present in other actual entities' (PR 50).

3. Finally, the prehended aspects are the marks that a past occasion of experience has imprinted upon a present one. This means that substances *can* be affected by other substances. Whitehead's substances have a passive, not solely an active side. Plato's definition of substance in the *Sophist* ('anything which possesses any sort of power to affect another, or to be affected by another even for a moment') is thereby fully vindicated.

The question now is whether this purified dynamic conception of substance helps us to understand the world we live in better than the traditional notion did. For certainly we experience change, but also order and stability. How can there be permanence in a world whose ultimate constituents are causally interacting process-units?

NOTES

1. As usual, it is to William James that one has to turn to find brilliant descriptions of our mental states. Here is a vibrant one from his *Essays in Radical Empiricism*: 'We live, as it were, upon the front edge of an advancing wave-crest, and our sense of a determinate direction in falling forward is all we cover of the future of our path' (ERE 69).
2. It is better to postpone the (legitimate) question whether this conception is vitiated by anthropomorphism; the point will be picked up later on in Chapter 7.
3. David Hume, *A Treatise of Human Nature*, ed. D. F. Norton and M. J. Norton, Oxford: Oxford University Press, 2000, p. 165 (= 1.4.6).
4. They are intelligently debated by John Lango in 'The Time of Whitehead's Concrescence', *Process Studies* 30/1, 2001, pp. 3–21.
5. The term was introduced by D. R. Griffin. One reason why it is better than 'panpsychism' is that it carries less misleading associations. As Griffin explains: '"Panpsychism" is the term that has generally been used . . . "Panexperientialism" is preferable, however, for two reasons: (1) The term "psyche" suggests that the basic units endure through long stretches of time, whereas they may be momentary experiences; and (2) "psyche" inevitably suggests a higher form of experience than would be appropriate for the most elementary units of nature' (*Unsnarling the World-Knot: Consciousness, Freedom and the Mind–Body Problem*, Berkeley:

University of California Press, p. 78). T. L. S. Sprigge, himself one of the most forceful advocates of panpsychism in the second half of the twentieth century, also uses the word 'panexperientialism', but in a different argumentative context and to refer to Bradley's view that Absolute Reality is a single encompassing cosmic experience. See his *James and Bradley: American Truth and British Reality*, Chicago: Open Court, 1993, p. 441.

PART III

From Process to Permanence

CHAPTER 6

Changing Shapes of Reality: Understanding Nature under a Social Analogy

FACT AND FORM

As described so far, Whitehead's universe of actual occasions is a world of sheer becoming. It is a Heraclitean cosmos in which 'all things flow'. As he puts it:

> Without doubt, if we are to go back to that ultimate, integral experience, unwarped by the sophistications of theory, that experience whose elucidation is the final aim of philosophy, the flux of things is one ultimate generalization around which we must weave our philosophical system. (PR 208)

Nevertheless, Whitehead is not oblivious of the fact that the world we inhabit is *also* a world of enduring objects:

> But there is a rival notion, antithetical to the former . . . This other notion dwells on permanences of things – the solid earth, the mountains, the stones, the Egyptian Pyramids, the spirit of man, God. (PR 208)

This rival notion is not entirely wrong. Even a mountain can be conceptualised as an event if one considers its existence within the horizon of millennia instead of years. But the mountain does not exist in a flash in the way that the momentary actual occasions do. And the same is true of all macroscopic entities of everyday life, chairs and tables for instance, as well as our own bodies; we do grow and decay, yet not all of a sudden.

In order to account for permanence, Whitehead introduces new ontological categories. The first relevant concept is that of *eternal object*. Among the basic categories of his system, he explains, 'actual entities and eternal objects stand out with a certain extreme finality' (PR 22).

'Eternal objects' is, roughly, Whitehead's designation for what are traditionally called Universals. In spite of his characterisation of Western philosophy as 'a series of footnotes to Plato' (PR 39), they are not conceived as ontologically independent entities like Plato's Ideas. Rather, they are conceived after the guise of Aristotle as the forms of things, that is to say, they are nothing apart from the concrete objects that instantiate them. The reason behind this choice should be obvious. As the difficulties Plato encountered in accounting for the notion of participation show,[1] the admission of a realm of Platonic Ideas existing parallel to the world of actualities would create a bifurcation as radical as the Cartesian division of the physical world into a realm of mind and a realm of matter. In terms of Whitehead's criteria, such a dualistic system would lack 'coherence'.

One main reason why Aristotelian Universals are called 'eternal objects' is that they are not bound to any particular time or place. While each occasion realises a quantum of space-time and is therefore not to be divorced from its position within the extensive continuum, Universals can occur at any moment at any place. They are 'eternal' in the sense that they are indifferent not to actualisation *per se*, but to the specific historical locus of their instantiation. There are many *red* things today; but there have certainly been many yesterday and there will be as many tomorrow.

But there is also a more substantial reason why Whitehead abandons the designation 'universal' in favour of 'eternal object'. On a traditional understanding, only Universals can be said to be 'present' in particular things. On Whitehead's revisionary conception of substance, however, particulars too can be said to enter into the constitution of other particulars. In this respect, the distinction between an actual entity and an eternal object does not quite match the distinction between a particular and a Universal. As he explains: 'every so-called "universal" is particular in the sense of being just what it is, diverse from everything else; and every so-called "particular" is universal in the sense of entering into the constitution of other actual entities' (PR 48). This is, it should be noticed, a small but clear example of the type of terminological shift that is required by revisionary metaphysics: even as venerable (and apparently innocuous) a word as 'universal' will have to be expunged from the new philosophical language.

THE SOCIAL THEORY OF NATURE

Another crucial category introduced by Whitehead to ground the possibility of permanence in a world of flux is that of *nexus*, by which Whitehead means any 'particular fact of togetherness among actual entities' (PR 20). The togetherness in question is, of course, the fact of relatedness that is realised when an actual occasion prehends another one.

A special class of nexuses is constituted when the actual occasions form a particularly cohesive group in virtue not merely of their prehensive relationships, but because they are able to sustain and to transmit to their successor occasions a common form (eternal object). Such nexuses are termed *societies* and can be of two types, according as to whether they are composed by a single historic route of actual occasions or by many such routes. The former type is called a *temporal* society, while the latter is designated (somewhat misleadingly, since each single occasion has a spatial as well as a temporal dimension) as *spatio-temporal*. What we are used to regarding as enduring things are really societies of occasions of one of these two types.

A fundamental physical entity like an electron or a proton, Whitehead speculates in *Process and Reality*, is a temporal society: it can be conceived as an historic route of occasions, a 'worm' of spatio-temporally extended momentary occurrences, each of which inherits from its predecessor a common form (PR 91). Another example of such a society is, for Whitehead, the soul of man, which consists of a single line of inheritance. Such societies can be termed 'personal', not in the sense that they have anything like conscious mentality, but in a sense closer to that expressed by the Latin *persona*: each such nexus 'sustains a character' (PR 35).

Macroscopic objects such as chairs and tables are, on the contrary, spatio-temporal societies. They are composed of many interacting streams that sustain a given structure over a longer period of time. On this account, the macroscopic objects of everyday life can be compared to colonies of insects or swarms of bees that move so quickly along the same patterned routes as to generate the incoercible impression of there being a permanent thing in front of us. Whitehead refers to such enduring things as 'corpuscular societies', an apt denomination that evokes unity, but also multiplicity and fragility associated with incumbent chaos and disorder.

The robust impression that societies make upon us in ordinary perception is such that some philosophers, like Aristoteles in the *Categories*, have misconceived these special types of nexuses for the paradigmatic substances:

> The real actual things that endure are all societies. They are not actual occasions. It is the mistake that has thwarted European metaphysics from the time of the Greeks, namely, to confuse societies with the completely real things which are the actual occasions. A society has an essential character, whereby it is the society that it is, and it has also accidental qualities which vary as circumstances alter. Thus a society, as a complete existence and as retaining the same metaphysical status, enjoys a history expressing its changing reactions to changing circumstances. But an actual occasion has no such history. It never changes. It only becomes and perishes. (AI 204)

As this passage makes clear, with the introduction of the concept of society the Aristotelian notion of an enduring thing endowed with essential and accident qualities is partially rescued. While it lacks ultimate validity, it can nevertheless be properly applied at that higher ontological level at which actual occasions group themselves into larger societal wholes.

Nature does not solely contain such things as rocks and mountains, however, but also living organisms: plants, the so-called 'lower' and 'higher' animals, and human beings. How are we to explain the differences between them? On the one hand, human societies are peculiarly clear instances of entities that persist even though their members change; no nineteenth-century Scot is alive today, yet Scotland has not passed away. On the other hand, human societies differ from one another in their internal organisation. The metaphysical moral that Whitehead draws is simple enough: different types of enduring objects must be differently structured.

In *Adventures of Ideas*, this idea is illustrated as follows:

> [W]hen we survey the living world, animal and vegetable, there are bodies of all types. Each living body is a society, which is not personal. But most of the animals, including all the vertebrates, seem to have their social system dominated by a subordinate society which is 'personal' . . . Thus in one sense a dog is a 'person', and in another sense he is a non-personal society. But the lower forms of animal life, and all vegetation, seem to lack the dominance of any included personal society. A tree is a democracy. (AI 206)

On this account, what distinguishes an inert enduring object such as a rock from a living organism such as a dog is that the latter possesses a hegemonic centre. A temporal society with personal order (what we would familiarly term the dog's 'soul' or 'mind') exerts control over the other parts of the larger spatio-temporal society within which it exists (the dog conceived as the union of its mind and the whole body). In the case of an inanimate object such as a rock, no such dominant unit has emerged. Lower animals and plants present still a different structure; in this case, no *single* dominant centre exists: many centres exert control over the organism within which they are embedded. Such organisms resemble 'democracies' rather than 'monarchies'.

Whitehead does not articulate his theory of nature in any great detail. He is careful, however, in explaining the basic principle upon which such a reconstruction will have to be attempted. Since on his view all basic constituents of reality are identical in fundamental essence, the differences between the complexes they form will have to be explained in terms of their different modes of organisation.

One reason why this structural principle is important is that it enables the panpsychist to counter an objection commonly raised against his theory. It is often rejected as ridiculous on the grounds that it forces one to ascribe experiences even to obviously inanimate objects such as rocks and chairs. It should be clear by now that Whitehead's theory has no such implication.[2] In the case of a compound entity such as a rock, for example, one has to distinguish between the experience of the *parts* (the actual occasions) and the experience of the *whole* (the rock). The fact that all of a rock's ultimate constituents are experiential does not imply that the rock *as such* has any experiences. Since in Whitehead's theory a rock lacks any dominant centre, the most one can say is that there is experience in its basic constituents.

This is still a perplexing view, but it is very different from the claim that ascribes experience to the rock itself. Stated in traditional logical terminology, to mistake one view for the other is to be guilty of the fallacy of composition – the error one incurs when one believes that all properties of the parts are *eo ipso* properties of the whole that they constitute (a rugby team is not a *man*, although each of the players is).

THE MIND–BODY PROBLEM: NON-CARTESIAN DUALISM

What view of human beings is entailed by Whitehead's social ontology? The division of societies into three main classes – those with one dominant centre (for example, a dog), those with more than one (a tree), and those with none (a rock) – provides the framework within which to address the mind–body problem.

Within this spectrum, a human being can only be viewed as a society in which the stream of experience that constitutes the enduring self has taken some significant amount of control over the remaining parts of the organism, especially of the brain. This leads to a peculiar form of dualism in which the mind is numerically distinct from the brain yet is also causally related to it. What distinguishes this form of dualism from Descartes's is the fact that the enduring object called 'mind' and the enduring object called 'body' are *numerically* yet not *qualitatively* different: they are both societies of actual occasions – the former being a temporal society, the latter a spatio-temporal one. The one obstacle that prevents understanding causal interaction, the heterogeneity of mind and matter, is therefore removed.

In *Process and Reality*, Whitehead writes:

> [I]n an animal body the presiding occasion, if there be one, is the final node, or intersection, of a complex structure of many enduring objects. Such a structure pervades the human body

> ... The human mind is thus conscious of its bodily inheritance ... This route of presiding occasions probably wanders from part to part of the brain, dissociated from the physical material atoms. (PR 109)

This theory may appear unsophisticated to the contemporary philosopher of mind, who would probably ask why Whitehead does not identify the mind with the brain instead of representing it, picturesquely, as 'wandering' within our heads. But consider what the suggested alternative would amount to within the context of Whitehead's metaphysics. Whitehead conceives of each of the ultimate physical particles constituting the body as a personal society, hence de facto as a kind of low-level mind. If the human mind were identical with the brain, then he would have to explain how the myriad experiences of such lower minds could ever give rise to the higher experiences of a human being.

How do the experiences in the neurons combine into the refined experience of a human being? This difficulty is nowadays called 'the combination problem'.[3] Rightly or wrongly, it is regarded by many as providing a conclusive refutation of any theory that ascribes a degree of experience to the basic constituents of nature.[4] In a passage of *The Principles of Psychology*, James had stated the problem thus:

> Take a sentence of a dozen words, and take twelve men and tell to each one word. Then stand the men in a row or jam them in a bunch, and let each think of his word as intently as he will; nowhere will there be a consciousness of the whole sentence. We talk of the 'spirit of the age,' and the 'sentiment of the people,' and in various ways we hypostatize 'public opinion.' But we know this to be symbolic speech, and never dream that the spirit, opinion, sentiment, etc., constitute a consciousness other than, and additional to, that of the several individuals whom the words 'age,' 'people,' or 'public' denote. The private minds do not agglomerate into a higher compound mind. (PP 160)

By drawing a numerical distinction between the mind and the brain, Whitehead sidesteps the problem here raised by James. He does not have to explain how 'private minds' could 'agglomerate into a higher compound mind'.

James's discussion of the compound mind in *The Principles of Psychology* must have strongly impressed Whitehead. At one point in *Process and Reality*, referring to the actualities that constitute living animal organisms, he writes:

> It is obvious that we must not demand another mentality presiding over these other actualities (a kind of Uncle Sam, over and above all the US citizens). All the life in the body is the life of the individual cells. There are thus millions upon millions of centres of life in each animal body. So what needs to be explained is not dissociation of personality but unifying control, by reason of which we not only have unified behaviour, which can be observed by others, but also consciousness of a unified experience. (PR 108)

Whitehead argues here that unified behaviour provides a sufficient criterion for ascribing to an organism a unified controlling instance. But how is this instance to be conceived? The solution Whitehead suggests is reached by means of an argument by analogy. The collection of all US citizens does not give rise to a new higher entity called 'Uncle Sam'. In the same way, the sum total of the bodily occasions does not yield a human mind. Whitehead does not develop the implication of this comparison any further. Nevertheless, it naturally leads to the theory of the mind as a presiding unity that he advocates. The ruling instance in the US is a citizen who has achieved a position of power. Analogously, the mind is one among the many constituents of the living organism that has come to occupy a favourable position within the system.

Whitehead's theory is closely reminiscent of Leibniz's doctrine of the mind as the body's dominant monad. Having renounced causal interaction, Leibniz can only interpret relations between monads in purely epistemic terms; according to him, what makes a monad A dominant over another monad B is the fact that A has clearer perceptions of B than B has of A. In Whitehead's metaphysics the reality of causal interaction is fully acknowledged and the notion of dominance obtains a more realistic interpretation. On the one hand, at least some bodily occasions are directly affected by the occasions that constitute the mind via the mechanism of prehension. On the other hand, the mind absorbs those very experiences that were just felt by the several parts of the body. To feel a pain in one's hand is on this view to experience (with some slight temporal delay) the very same pain that was felt by the occasions making up the hand.

It is not that we merely localise the pain in a certain region of the body. The pain was originally felt *by the occasions in the hand*, and only secondarily *by us*. The human body, Whitehead remarks,

> is a set of occasions miraculously coordinated so as to pour its inheritance into various regions within the brain. There is thus every reason to believe that our sense of unity with the body *has the same original as our sense of unity with our immediate past of personal experience.* (AI 189; my emphasis)

Although this theory sounds fantastic, it is difficult to deny that it has a strong phenomenological appeal. For we all feel that – in a way most of us would find it difficult to articulate precisely – we both *are* and *are not* identical with our bodies. When we are ill we look at our body as a part of ourselves as well as an alien presence; the body then becomes what we try to preserve, but also what we are fighting against. Another example: as time passes by, we feel that our body, which we could so easily command in younger years, increasingly becomes alienated from us. The body seems to gain a sort of independent life, as if it were trying to restore its own rights against our commanding powers. Our natural yet deeply perplexing sense of bodily intimacy squares with Whitehead's doctrine that we are *numerically distinct* from the bodily occasions yet *constituted* by aspects of them. As Whitehead nicely puts it, '[t]here are animal bodies as well as animal minds; and in our experience such minds always occur incorporated' (AI 205).

Incidentally, Whitehead observes, our ordinary modes of talk also bear witness to the notion that our bodily organs are themselves sentient. We say that our *hands* 'hurt', not our brains, firing neurons or disembodied Cartesian minds. Ordinary language is not solely suggestive of a bad metaphysics because of its grammatical structures; it is also a reliable 'storehouse' (PR 5, 10–11) of important philosophical knowledge.

THE RIDDLE OF PERSONAL IDENTITY

What seems problematic is not Whitehead's explanation of the union of mind and body, but his explanation of the status of the mind as an enduring entity. Consider, for example, the following account of the thinking subject:

> The simplest example of a society in which the successive nexus of its progressive realization have a common extensive pattern is when each such nexus is purely temporal and continuous. The society, in each stage of realization, then consists of a set of contiguous occasions in serial order. A man, defined as an enduring percipient, is such a society. This definition of a man is exactly what Descartes means by a thinking substance. (AI 205)

As we have seen in Chapter 3, in *Process and Reality* Whitehead charges Descartes with the mistake of conceiving of the subject under the category of substance. In this passage, he now concedes that Descartes's view of the soul is more similar to his own than appears at first sight. The Cartesian notion of a constant creation (the medieval *creatio continua*), he argues, does indeed entail that human subjectivity comes in pulses: 'It will be remembered,' Whitehead explains, 'that [for Descartes] endurance is nothing else than successive re-creation by God. Thus the Cartesian conception of the human soul and that here put forward differ only in the function assigned to God. Both conceptions involve a succession of occasions, each with its own measure of immediate completeness' (AI 205). In this connection, Whitehead could have also quoted Leibniz, who in the *Monadology* writes that 'all created or derivative monads are products, and are generated, so to speak, by continual fulgurations of the divinity from moment to moment' (AG 219, §47). The word 'fulguration' is one capable of firing a philosopher's imagination, and could indeed very well be used to qualify the mode of existence of an actual occasion.

But how compelling is Whitehead's own explanation of the enduring self as a series of experiential events? If each occasion 'comes with its own measure of immediate completeness' (that is to say, each is a genuinely new creation), what makes the identity of a person over time? The concept of the self as an underlying substance did provide a clear answer to this riddle. But once the conception of an underlying substance is rejected, the question immediately arises: what prevents the unitary self from dissolving into a plurality of distinct momentary selves? What is, in other words, their ground of union?

This problem, of which Whitehead is fully aware, becomes dramatic if one also considers the intricate, interconnected nature of his process universe. In *Adventures of Ideas*, he writes:

> our consciousness of the self-identity pervading our life-thread of occasions, is nothing other than knowledge of a special strand of unity within the general unity of nature. It is a locus within the whole, marked out by its own peculiarities, but otherwise exhibiting the general principle which guides the constitution of the whole. This general principle is the object-to-subject structure of experience . . . it can be conceived as the doctrine of the immanence of the past energizing in the present. (AI 187–8)

As this passage indicates, a human occasion of experience is in some sense aware of belonging to a given causal stream, *as opposed to all other streams existing in nature*. This is a surprising fact in an organically connected universe like that envisioned by Whitehead, for here each occasion inherits not solely from its immediate ancestor, but also from occasions belonging to other streams. Nevertheless, only the occasions belonging to *one* specific stream are felt as constituting our previous life.

Whitehead makes several distinct suggestions to meet this challenge. One way to account for the problem is to assume that the present moment 'sums up' (prehends) more of the contents of its predecessor occasions in its own personal stream than of the contents of any other past actualities. Such an explanation is not entirely convincing, however. Experiential shocks (a bomb exploding near us, a sudden and painful fall on to the ground, the incredibly loud beginning of a rock concert) provide interesting illustrations. The experiential continuity is here almost completely broken, as new contents suddenly enter the mind from the outside – 'filling' it entirely anew, as it were. Nevertheless, this hardly affects our personal identity; although the mind has been filled with new experiences, we both *remain* the very same persons and are *aware* of having remained such. (In some extreme cases, one may lose for a while the sense of one's own identity; one does not, however, thereby turn into another person.) The crucial consideration here is that a radical break in experiential continuity is not identical with, nor does it necessarily entail, a change in personal identity.

By calling the self a 'personal society' (that is to say, one which 'sustains a character'), Whitehead is also implying that a common form is transmitted from one occasion to the next; there is within such a society a linearly propagated defining characteristic. This account is not very convincing either. An explanation of endurance in terms of momentary events and a recurring pattern sounds plausible with respect to objects such as electrons and protons, but it lacks all evidence when the nature of the self is at stake. According to Whitehead, '[t]he only strictly personal society of which we have direct discriminative intuition is the society of our own personal experiences' (AI 206). But I am hardly aware of there being a common pattern or form that remains identical throughout all – or even only a significant portion of – my experiential states. Contrary to other tenets in Whitehead's philosophy, this specific one does not have much support in our phenomenology.

But why, it could be asked, should one expect the ground of personal identity to show up phenomenally? True, there is no reason why this should be the case. Whitehead's characteristic procedure of turning phenomenological conceptions into metaphysical ones does, however, create such an expectation.

Another aspect of the passage quoted above deserves consideration. Whitehead states there that our sense of personal identity is our awareness of belonging to a definite strand of occasions within the larger stream of nature. This suggests that, according to him, we always have *some sense (however vague it may be) of our causal origin*. Now, within the framework of the pulse-theory of the self, the problem of personal identity is really the problem of explaining the deeper connection that exists between the present moment of experience and the previous one in the series constituting the self. Somehow, our present moment of experience must be more firmly 'anchored' to the occasions constituting our own life-thread than it is to the occasions constituting other natural threads. How can we understand this 'strong' linkage?

One answer could run as follows. As explained in Chapter 5, Whitehead's actual occasions achieve completion as the result of a (pretemporal) process called concrescence. Why not speculate that the present occasion literally *originates* out of its predecessor occasion? Why not postulate that each occasion, while perishing, 'ejects' a first experiential nucleus around which the new subject begins to grow? On this view, the very early phase of the concrescence would consist in a kind of 'reduplication' of the occasion just gone. In later phases of the concrescence, this initial core would then be successively modified, until a new moment of experience is fully formed. This could (but need not) be what Whitehead means in the last long passage quoted above when he says that 'the object-to-subject structure of experience' can also be expressed as 'the doctrine of the immanence of the past *energizing* in the present' (AI 187–8; my emphasis).

As a matter of fact, Whitehead does at times propose yet another explanation. According to this, each satisfied occasion comes with what may be called a characteristic 'emotional' tone. It is this emotional tonality that, at least in the early phases of the concrescence, is reproduced within the emerging occasion. What links a present moment of experience (be it human or non-human) to its immediate antecedent within an experiential series is, on this account, something comparable to a feeling of sympathy. At one point, Whitehead makes the point thus: 'There is . . . an analogy between the transference of energy from particular occasion to particular occasion in physical nature and the transference of affective tone, with its emotional energy, from one occasion to another in any human personality' (AI 188). This explanation is highly speculative, of course, not just because of the identity here suggested between physical energy and human emotion. The main problem is that the concrescence, if there is any such thing at all, belongs to a realm of reality lying beyond all immediate observation and verification. How can we possibly know what is happening in this pre-temporal realm? To the best of my knowledge, Whitehead never addresses this objection – that is to say, he never explains how to safely dig into the concrescence's mysterious depths. As a consequence, all claims about the concrescence's inner structure have to be regarded as arbitrary. This does not turn his proposed solution into a straightforward absurdity, of course; nevertheless, one does not quite see why it should be accepted.

Before bringing this section to an end, another way in which the problem of personal identity arises within Whitehead's metaphysics should be briefly considered. So far, we have been discussing the relation that the present entertains with previous moments of experience. What about the connection between the present self and the occasions that will enter its personal stream in the future, that is to say, our future momentary selves? If one holds that the self comes in successive pulses, it is legitimate to ask why my present self should be more concerned about my future momentary selves than about the future selves of other individuals. Why do I have a kind of 'anticipatory sympathy' towards those occasions that will become (but at the moment are not, being as yet non-existent) components of my own life-history? From the perspective of the present occasions *all* future occasions are novel entities, but we hardly take a neutral stance towards them, my future selves being more valuable to me than the future selves of, say, any of my neighbours. Whitehead's pulse-theory stands somewhat at odds with this kind of egoistic concern for our future moments of experience.

THE NATURAL ORDER OF THINGS

The permanence of the empirical world does not concern solely the existence of relatively enduring things such as rocks, animals and human beings, but the equally undeniable existence of regularities. What is the metaphysical status of natural laws? Whitehead's position may be usefully contrasted with the one provided by seventeenth-century materialism. According to this cosmological view, natural laws (1) are imposed *ab extra* by a divine Mind and (2) are valid without exception for the entire natural realm; they are, in other words, entirely deterministic. This conception, basically Newton's clockwork universe, is the sole one that is compatible with the notion that the basic constituents of reality are ontologically self-subsistent. On this basis, the relations between substances can only be 'external', in the sense that the *ground* of their holding cannot lie in the natures of the related substances. Hence, if the substance-like material atoms turn out to be related after all, then the reason why they are so must be looked for in some principle lying outside the nature of objects.

All this immediately leads to a view of laws as imposed by an external agency, namely God. Of course, one could try to escape this Deistic conclusion by arguing that natural laws are only descriptions of observed regularities. But once again, this positivistic doctrine would just be a subterfuge for avoiding difficult metaphysical questions. If the regularities can be described, as the Positivist admits, this is because they are, in some sense, a fact. And for the speculative mind – animated as it is by the faith that reality is not inscrutable to reason – all facts call for an explanation.

Whitehead's rejection of the doctrine of imposed laws parallels his critique of the doctrine of vacuous actualities. There are plain facts of our experience that the theory does not account for; as any farmer knows, nature is not only regular, but capricious as well. It is the entire wisdom of humanity, as gathered in myths and legends, undistorted by philosophical rationalisations, that tells this tale: 'We inherit legends, weird, horrible, beautiful, expressing in curious, specialized ways the interweaving of law and capriciousness in the mystery of things' (AI 111). Admittedly, this may look like a blatant confusion of epistemic and metaphysical indeterminacy; the fact that natural things *seem* 'capricious' (that is to say, not acting according to a fixed rule) does not imply that they also *are* such.

Can it be that a great philosopher has failed to take notice of a very trivial distinction? Certainly not; the point of appealing to the primitive experiences of humankind is not to secure a metaphysical thesis, but to slowly *prepare* our minds, so that they can be open, more fully receptive to a different vision of things. One main difficulty in reading Whitehead is precisely this: understanding comes with the realisation that his writings are not just collections of arguments meant to establish a conclusion, although they are this as well. Rather, many of his remarks have the character of *aperçus*, whose aim is to perplex the reader and thereby 'deconstruct' his or her established way of thinking. In order to achieve this end – the regaining, one could say, of a kind of philosophical naivety – Whitehead does not hesitate to be trivial and, sometimes, even to disregard scholarly conventions and well-known distinctions.

The doctrine of deterministic laws, Whitehead goes on to explain, has been made obsolete by the most recent scientific insights. Natural laws hold for larger aggregates, not for individual particles, which may deviate from the common course. '[A]n individual electron is a rare bird whose behavior is unpredictable: our information about electrons mostly concerns flocks numbering millions' (AI 115). Contrary to what the word 'law' so strongly suggests, natural laws are not expressions of divine decrees, but statistical generalisations.[5] In *Adventures of Ideas*, the point is made thus: 'In so far as we are merely interested in a confused result of many instances, then the law can be said to have a statistical character. It is now the opinion of physicists that most of the laws of physics, as known in the nineteenth century, are of this character' (AI 112).

Based on this account, what is needed is not so much an explanation of exceptionless regularity, but of the *coexistence* of order and disorder. The social theory of nature outlined in the previous section provides an ideal matrix for fulfilling this explanatory task. On this view, each actual occasion is conceived as possessing a quantum of spontaneity, since the process of concrescence issues in a non-deterministic synthesis of causal data. Insofar as each occasion enters into the constitution of a larger societal whole, it now becomes possible to speculate, such a natural spontaneity may come to be inhibited by the pressure exerted upon it by its fellow occasions.

Human societies provide apt terms for comparison. As there are societies paralysed by adherence to ancient customs, so there are wholly inert things such as rocks and tables. These objects can be conceived as being constituted by occasions entirely unable to break the spell of inherited custom. In such societies, some particle may deviate from the general rule; still, its anomalous conduct would fail to have any effect upon the whole because of the passivity of the remaining particles. On the contrary, in societies where one or more member has acquired a position of relative dominance and independence, or in nexuses where no definite order has yet emerged, one could expect the anomalous conduct of some one member to have an impact upon the behaviour of the whole. This is, indeed, what happens with human beings and the higher animals, whose behaviour can never be fully predicted.

Whitehead's rejection of the traditional conception of law has some startling implications. On the social theory of nature, laws originate from the very bottom of things. They record the behaviour that is characteristic of the main types of societies, not of each single constituent of them. Conceived as functions of the behaviour of the worldly occasions, natural laws must also be conceived as changing with the behaviour of the occasions constituting the societies for which they hold. This means that the present order of nature is not eternally valid, but that it is itself the result of an *evolutionary* process. Natural laws do not make evolution possible, but emerge in the course of it: '[T]he modern evolutionary view of the physical universe should conceive of the laws of nature as evolving concurrently with the things constituting the environment' (AI 112). Although this is very difficult for us to imagine, the possibility that the current order of things may change in the future is indeed open. The stream of consciousness comes in successive pulses of experience. Analogously, Whitehead's universe goes through a series of successive 'epochs', each epoch being characterised by its own peculiar social organisation and type of order.

WHAT KEEPS ALL THINGS GOING?

Whitehead labelled the complex of his metaphysical doctrines 'the philosophy of organism', and referred to *Process and Reality* as an 'essay in cosmology' (humbly, because to call such an impressive book an 'essay' is to suggest that it is only a tentative sketch).[6] In fact, the view of the cosmos that emerges from his speculations in this book is that of a large organic whole, an organism harbouring within itself infinite smaller organisms of infinite different types. On this theory, each of the less specialised societies constitutes a supportive environment within which the smaller, more specialised societies can flourish. This is true of a human being as well; there could be nothing so refined as a human mind apart from the environment constituted by the brain, which in turn requires the supporting environment of the rest of the body.

As Whitehead understands it, nature is a society of societies. There are hierarchies of complexity within it, which makes the emergence of higher forms of mentality possible. Once again, Leibniz is never far from Whitehead's mind. Leibnizian conceptions are ably fused with notions derived from the theory of evolution and contemporary physics. In fact, the entire social theory of nature reads like a vast commentary on some striking passages in Leibniz's *Monadology*:

> there is a world of creatures, of living beings, of animals, of entelechies, of souls in the least part of matter. Each portion of matter can be conceived as a garden full of plants, and as a

pond full of fish. But each branch of a plant, each limb of an animal, each drop of its humors, is still another such garden or pond. And although the earth and air lying between the garden plants, or the water lying between the fish of the pond, are neither plant nor fish, they contain yet more of them, though of a subtleness imperceptible to us, most often. (AG 222, §§66–8)

This is a very good description of Whitehead's social universe as well. However, Whitehead lacks the infinity-thought; nature as he conceives it is not divisible into organisms *ad infinitum*: at some point, one reaches the ultimate level of actual occasions.

What Whitehead also adds to this Leibnizian picture of the natural world is a Heraclitean, one could even say 'anarchistic', touch. Not all occasions need to be incorporated within any stable society (cf. PR 110), nor are there well-defined borders between one society and another. When we breathe, molecules from the surrounding environment enter our bodies; are they part of ourselves or are they not? There is for Whitehead no proper answer to this question, identity and difference being often only relative concepts. Furthermore, societies are not only reciprocally supportive, but also enter into competition with one another; no natural being is exempted from the painful struggle for life. Finally, within the larger whole of nature, transiency and fluency are everywhere. Everything is in continuous evolution, each established arrangement being only a fragile, provisory achievement. As Whitehead puts it in one of his more apocalyptic (perhaps only playful?) moods, we could conceive of a 'vast upheaval of nature' (PR 43) shattering into fragments even as solid a construction as Edinburgh's Castle Rock.

But why doesn't the universe ever achieve a final, definite state? What keeps all things constantly going? Whitehead answers this question by reference to the concept of creativity. As he puts it:

In all philosophic theory there is an ultimate which is actual in virtue of its accidents. It is only then capable of characterization through its accidental embodiments, and apart from these accidents is devoid of actuality. In the philosophy of organism this ultimate is termed 'creativity'. . . (PR 7)

Thus, *creativity* is the final principle that propels the universe forward. It is at work in the two basic processes that animate Whitehead's universe, the *transition* from one actual occasion to another and the *concrescence* in the course of which a novel occasion comes into being. But creativity is not to be conceived after the guise of an eminent divine principle. It is best compared to Spinoza's God (whose essence is said to be power in the *Ethics*), yet deprived of any substantial reality:

> In monistic philosophies, Spinoza's or absolute idealism, this ultimate is God, who is also equivalently termed 'The Absolute.' In such monistic schemes, the ultimate is illegitimately allowed a final, 'eminent' reality, beyond that ascribed to any of its accidents. (PR 7)

In Whitehead's metaphysical scheme, only the many 'accidents' are real, that is, the actual occasions. The one substance dissolves into the universal creative urge that permeates them all. Even materialists, Whitehead argues in *Adventures of Ideas*, are bound to recognise an eminent reality. In a materialistic worldview, a transcendent God is required to set the atoms in motion. In Whitehead's process philosophy of nature, no such *deus ex machina* is needed. Given his rejection of the traditional conception of substance as statically enduring, he can freely postulate a *nisus* towards change and novelty immanent in the nature of things. There is little than can be said upon this fundamental fact. We simply have to acknowledge it as such.

Is such an appeal to a brute fact acceptable? Philosophy begins in wonder, Aristotle observes in the first book of the *Metaphysics*, a wonder that disappears when everything has been completely explained. As against such an overinflated rationalistic ambition, Whitehead contends, wonder always remains.

NOTES

1. For a clear analysis of these difficulties, which Plato himself articulated in his *Parmenides*, see J. Moravcsik, *Plato and Platonism*, Oxford: Blackwell, 1992, especially pp. 129–68.

2. Some forms of panpsychism may, however, have this implication. See, for example, the discussion of Spinoza's panpsychism in D. Skrbina, *Panpsychism in the West*, Cambridge, MA: MIT Press, 2005, pp. 87–91, and M. Della Rocca, *Spinoza*, London and New York: Routledge, 2008, pp. 108–18. In *The Conscious Mind: In Search of a Fundamental Theory*, Oxford: Oxford University Press, 1996, D. Chalmers notoriously speculates that there might be a 'what-it-is-like-to-be-a-thermostat' (p. 286). This is, admittedly, not the best way to make panpsychism look attractive.
3. This denomination was introduced by William Seager in 'Consciousness, Information, and Panpsychism', *Journal of Consciousness Studies* 2, 1995, pp. 272–88.
4. Possibly wrongly, for it is all but clear that the notion of mental combination is incoherent. For a discussion of this point, see P. Basile, 'It Must Be True – But How Can it Be? Some Remarks on Panpsychism and Mental Composition', in P. Basile et al. (eds), *The Metaphysics of Consciousness*, Cambridge: Cambridge University Press, 2010, pp. 93–112. Nagel holds a slightly optimistic position in *The View from Nowhere*, Oxford: Oxford University Press, 1986: 'The combinatorial problem and the apparent outlandishness of ascribing "mental" properties to carbon atoms,' he writes, 'are aspects of a single conceptual difficulty. We cannot at present understand how a mental event could be composed of myriad smaller proto-mental events on the model of our understanding of how a muscle movement is composed of myriad physico-chemical events at the molecular level. We lack the concept of a mental part-whole relation' (p. 50). If I am not mistaken, Nagel does not exclude here that we may one day come to possess such a concept.
5. This view was not new in 1929, however, as it had been already advocated by C. S. Peirce in his 'The Architecture of Theories', *The Monist*, 1891, pp. 161–76. To the best of my knowledge, Whitehead never mentions the founder of pragmatism in his metaphysical writings. Whitehead's colleague at Cambridge, James Ward, does, however, refer to this particular paper as providing a clear example of the most advanced metaphysical research in Chapter IV ('The Contingency of the World') of his *Realm of Ends or Pluralism and Theism*, Cambridge: Cambridge University Press, 1911, p. 170.

6. Unfortunately, Whiteheadians tend to lose sight of this fact at times. Writing about Whitehead in 1957, John Passmore observed: 'There are those who would maintain that he is the outstanding philosopher of our century – even if there are others who would dismiss his metaphysical constructions as obscure private dreams' (*A Hundred Years of Philosophy*, London: Penguin, 1957, p. 335). If the overall argument of this essay is sound, then both attitudes are deeply mistaken.

CHAPTER 7

Theological Afterthoughts: A Neo-Platonic God for a Darwinian Universe?

MAKING SENSE OF RELIGIOUS EXPERIENCE

Whitehead's concept of experience is larger than the scientific one, since it includes the religious experiences of humankind. These are not difficult to accommodate within Whitehead's conception of nature, according to which we live literally immersed in an ocean of feeling. Consider the human body, which Whitehead describes as a society harbouring myriad other smaller societies, each of which is in turn constituted by myriad mind-like entities. It may look like a wild speculation, of course, but in the same way in which a bodily cell or a neuron has a relation to our mind, so could our mind stand in relation to one or more high-level minds. We may never realise this. Occasionally, however, our ordinary awareness may rise to a more or less clear consciousness of such higher mental presences, none of which needs to be identified with God. It would seem therefore that nothing compels Whitehead to introduce a Deity into his metaphysics. Nature could be conceived as a self-organising whole, one that gives rise in the course of evolution to new layers of increasing social complexity. And with the increase of complexity, higher levels of mentality could be achieved.

This is not Whitehead's conclusion. He does indeed forcefully reject the view of God as an all-powerful, omniscient, perfect being; this theology, he contends (PR 343), has been once and for all refuted by Hume in his *Dialogues Concerning Natural Religion* (1779). But there are undeniable facts of our experience, he also urges us to consider, that can be accounted for only by postulating some kind of extra-worldly, divine Reality.

NOVELTY AND ORDER REVISITED: TWO THEISTIC ARGUMENTS

In order to show that a process theory of nature needs to be supplemented by a process theory of God, Whitehead appeals to two main arguments. God first enters his system with what appears to be a veritable *coup de théâtre* towards the middle of *Process and Reality*. The following passage is long and difficult; because of its importance, however, it deserves to be quoted in full:

> The question, how, and in what sense, one unrealized eternal object can be more, or less, proximate to an eternal object in realized ingression – that is to say, in comparison with any other unfelt eternal object – is left unanswered . . . In conformity with the ontological principle, this question can be answered only by reference to some actual entity. Every eternal object has entered into the conceptual feelings of God. Thus, a more fundamental account must ascribe the reverted conceptual feeling in a temporal subject to its conceptual feeling derived . . . from the hybrid physical feeling of the relevancies conceptually ordered in God's experience. In this way, by the recognition of God's characterization of the creative act, a more complete rational explanation is attained. The Category of Reversion is then abolished . . . (PR 249–50)

Let us begin by considering the problem raised here by Whitehead. At this stage of his argument, he has already expounded his social theory of nature. The theory is not abandoned, but a doubt is raised as to its ultimate validity. Specifically, given that new Forms constantly appear in the course of evolution, where do they come from? Within an enduring personal society, the novel actual occasion inherits a Form instantiated by the preceding occasions. Nevertheless, the nexus is not conceived deterministically; new Forms may enter the concrescence and become ingredients of the satisfied occasion. As the passage suggests, Whitehead had initially thought of introducing a concept ('the Category of Reversion') in order to account for this shift. But Whitehead now recognises that this will not suffice. If the only Forms available to the concrescence come from the past, an occasion could introduce a Form not previously instantiated by any of the occasions of the society to which it belongs. Nevertheless, such a Form would not be 'new' in an absolute sense of the word, since it would have to be derived from some actuality already in existence. Thus, Whitehead concludes, the problem of accounting for the reality of novelties is not solved merely by granting occasions a capacity for 'Reversion', that is to say, a capacity to instantiate Forms different from those instantiated by the other occasions in the social nexus. A more radical explanation is needed.

Whitehead solves the difficulty by an appeal to the neo-Platonic notion of God as a depository of Forms. All Forms, realised as well as unrealised, are said to be contained in the unity of God's eternal vision: '[E]ternal objects, as in God's primordial nature, constitute the Platonic world of ideas' (PR 46). Whenever a new Form makes its ingression into the world, this is because some worldly occasion has derived it from an immediate grasp of the divine Intellect. Such a 'grasp' is referred to by Whitehead in the passage quoted above as a 'hybrid physical feeling' – the feeling being 'hybrid' because what is prehended is indeed a Form, yet not as existing *per se* but as subsistent in God. Forms, one could say, are not directly apprehended, but 'abstracted' through a direct experience of God.

Whitehead's second argument for the existence of God is based upon a reconsideration of the status of natural laws. Whitehead is surprised that evolution should have given rise to so many orderly structures. In his view, this is hard to explain solely in terms of Darwinian concepts. Other agencies must be at work besides wild natural forces. The notion of natural laws as immanent is not false, he concludes, but needs to be counterbalanced by some notion of imposition. As he has it:

> apart from some notion of imposed Law, the doctrine of immanence provides absolutely no reason why the universe should not be steadily relapsing into lawless chaos. In fact, the Universe, as understood in accordance with the doctrine of Immanence, should exhibit itself as including a stable actuality whose mutual implication with the remainder of things secures an inevitable trend towards order. The Platonic 'persuasion' is required. (AI 115)

The previous argument is a legitimate attempt to make the categories of *Process and Reality* consistent with the fact of evolutionary novelty. This one verges on the sophistical. Is it so obvious that nature displays an inevitable trend towards order? Whitehead does not, at any rate, say anything to justify this optimistic claim.

The argument does have a certain *prima facie* plausibility if limited to the human realm, though. Certainly, many of the things we most cherish (including art, literature and philosophy) have little survival value. Although this is controversial,[1] it would seem that only a Nietzschean *Übermensch* could flourish in a society exclusively ruled by Darwinian principles. A survey of human history, Whitehead argues in *Adventures of Ideas*, reveals on the contrary that there has been moral as well as technological and economic progress. Specifically, Whitehead contends, in the course of history human beings have acquired an 'increased sense of the dignity of man, as man. There has been a growth, slow and wavering, of respect for the preciousness of human life. This is the humanitarian spirit, gradually emerging in the slow sunrise of a thousand years' (AI 83). If this is granted, then an explanation is needed as to what makes civilised forms of life possible.

But how is the new doctrine of imposition to be understood? What is meant by 'Platonic' persuasion? As the world develops, Whitehead further speculates, God elaborates a plan as to what is the best order to be realised. Consistent with this plan, a Form is presented to each worldly occasion as an ideal worthy of realisation. While it is still in the process of becoming, the occasion may freely 'decide' whether to accept it or not. Needless to say, the greater the number of occasions following God's invitation, the greater the order that nature will display, that is to say, the more it will approximate to being a 'cosmos', an orderly as well as a beautiful whole. On this view, God is not a ruler any more, but a great persuasive force. He tries to lead the world in one favoured direction, yet he does not compel it.

One notable feature of this view is that God and the world are conceived as evolving *pari passu*. There is no final end towards which God strives to lead the world. He is engaged in the never-ending task of ordering and evaluating Forms in order to create new schemes of ideals to be presented to the worldly actualities. God's proposal to the world is (in a sense to be considered shortly) 'the best', yet not absolutely but solely with respect to a particular historic juncture. Given the state of the world at any given moment, following God's proposal would lead to the best *realisable* (as opposed to 'abstractly conceivable') outcome.

This is a surprising doctrine. As we have seen, Whitehead devotes the early pages of *Process and Reality* to the requirements that speculative metaphysics must satisfy in order to remain intellectually responsible. But it is difficult not to regard this theory of divine intervention as a suggestive, yet free speculative fancy. In formulating it, moreover, Whitehead ascribes to the worldly occasions a capacity for taking decisions and evaluating alternatives that only a human being could possibly have. One can imagine Newton's material atoms being moved around in empty space by forces activated by a divine architect. But it is difficult to think of the occasions entering into the constitution of a cell, an atom or an electron responding to the divine call. There is such a thing as moral or religious conscience in human beings, but the phenomenon can hardly be universalised. Undoubtedly, the otherwise respectable doctrine of panpsychism does here degenerate into a kind of primitive animism or anthropomorphism.

THE HIGHER PHASES OF EXPERIENCE: EMERGENCE REVISITED

This is not the only juncture at which the charge of anthropomorphism may be raised against Whitehead's theory of actual occasions. As against panpsychism, it is sometimes argued that nothing is really solved by ascribing experiences to the basic constituents of reality. Even admitting that it makes sense to postulate that the ultimate constituents of things have feelings, how do we explain the origination of the higher mental states characteristic of human beings?

One critic has made the point thus:

> Can it be consistent dogmatically to deny the possibility
> of the conscious having developed out of the unconscious
> (in the sense of the totally unfeeling), and yet to assert
> the development of the humanly intelligent out of what is
> quite incapable of reasoning? If we are to reject the former
> supposition on the ground of unintelligibility, it seems we
> ought to reject the latter too.[2]

This is, I submit, a powerful challenge. Primitive mental states such as an emotion or a pleasurable sensation do indeed seem to be *qualitatively* different from mental states such as, say, our grasping a mathematical truth. A similar point may be raised with respect to other more refined types of mental states. How are we to explain, for instance, the origination of moral consciousness out of brute immediate feelings? Even the pan-experientialist, so the argument goes, has to face (his own version of) the heterogeneity problem.

Whitehead's metaphysic provides the resources, if not for meeting this challenge conclusively, then at least for sketching a solution. If the reality of a neo-Platonic God is assumed, the transition from the lower to the higher phases of experience can be made sense of. On this theological basis, moral and mathematical knowledge can be interpreted as a peculiar type of experience – one whose objects are ideas and truths deposited in God's eternal mind. On this view, what one has to postulate beside God is a capacity for grasping abstract objects in the actual occasion, and this is precisely what Whitehead does with his concept of a 'conceptual' prehension.

There is, however, a loose end to this solution. For since all occasions are identical in fundamental nature, it now turns out that even the occasions entering into the constitution of such basic physical entities as electrons and protons must possess a capacity for grasping abstract objects; de facto, they are all endowed with a little mind or proto-intellect. Once again, Whitehead's actual occasions turn out to be more human-like than one would have wished them to be.

GOD'S CONSEQUENT NATURE

In his discussion of Leibniz's theory of pre-established harmony, Whitehead expresses surprise that Leibniz could conceive of his God as a causally active substance. God cannot be an exception to the basic ontological principles, but must be their chief exemplification. In Whitehead's theory, substances have an active as well as a passive side; they leave a mark upon later occasions but are also affected by previous ones. This same duplicity must now be ascribed to God as well. This line of reasoning leads Whitehead to conceive of his God as 'dipolar', namely, as possessing a 'primordial' as well as a 'consequent' nature. While the former coincides, as we have just seen, with God's envisaging of the Forms, the latter consists in God's capacity to absorb all worldly actualities. God is not solely a cosmic intellect and a repository of all possible Forms, but a cosmic memory and a deposit for all realised actualities as well. What has become past does not simply vanish, but continues its existence as 'objectified' within God's experience.

The notion of God's consequent or 'physical' nature raises two serious difficulties. For one thing, past occasions are said to be objectified in their completeness. Unless particulars possess something like a capability of occurring in more than one place at the same time, a characteristic traditionally reserved for Universals, it is hard to see how aspects of them could also survive in worldly actualities. Secondly, Whitehead says that in God's consequent nature actual occasions are arranged and transmuted. The general difficulty that plagues the theory of prehension – how can an experience remain numerically identical if it changes its qualitative feel – arises here once again. For the 'transmuted' experience objectified in God must surely be different from the original one.

In addition to these two difficulties, a rather strange epistemological puzzle arises. If my experiences are absorbed in God's nature in their entirety, but in a transmuted form, how do I know that they have not been transmuted already and that I am not in God now? Of course, it doesn't seem to me to be so; but what precisely puts me in a position to say so?[3]

Somewhat surprising – but also theologically innovative – is the following description of God's consequent nature:

> The truth itself is nothing else than how the composite
> natures of the organic actualities of the world obtain adequate
> representation in the divine nature. Such representations
> compose the 'consequent nature' of God, which evolves in its
> relationship to the evolving world . . . (PR 12)

As the world develops, the past actualities are summed up in God, where they are fused together into a single representation of the entire cosmic history – 'the truth itself'. Since history never comes to a stop, new occasions enter God's consequent nature, so that the synoptic representation contained there is constantly updated. God is in a way omniscient, yet only *ex post*; since history exists in the making, not even God can have any knowledge of future events. There simply are no such events to be known in the first place. In this respect, Whitehead's God differs significantly from Leibniz's and from the God of classical theism, as he neither knows the individual essences of particular things (what he is aware of in his Intellect are solely Platonic Forms) nor the truth-value of any future contingent.

HOW GOOD IS WHITEHEAD'S GOD?

Whitehead particularly emphasises the fact that, because of his new understanding of the concept of substance as a passive/active unity, he is in a position to provide a better rationale for traditional religious images, especially biblical ones. This is one of Whitehead's best-known descriptions of God's consequent nature:

> The consequent nature of God is his judgment on the world. He saves the world as it passes into the immediacy of his own life. It is the judgment of a tenderness which loses nothing that can be saved. It is also the judgment of a wisdom which uses what in the temporal world is mere wreckage. (PR 346)

Insofar as God is affected by the world, for example, he can be said to be 'the great companion – the fellow-sufferer who understands' (PR 351). And insofar as he proposes his chosen Form to the worldly occasions without forcing them into acceptance, he can be thought of as a caring, loving father. On a traditional understanding of substance as a perfect and causally self-contained entity, on the contrary, it becomes impossible to understand why God should be concerned with the world's fate. A God such as Aristotle's unmoved mover, for example, does not care about the world; it is the world that 'loves' him, striving to become as God-like as it can. Furthermore, and the point is really worth making, the notion that all happenings are gathered in God's consequent nature may encourage human beings to deal with difficult circumstances in the most honourable way. The thought that whatever value we have achieved is not lost forever, but is saved as an eternal ingredient in God's consequent nature, is such as to infuse new life and enthusiasm into a depressed soul. Such a view is likely to produce 'a quality of mind steady in its reliance that fine action is treasured in the nature of things' (AI 274).

Undoubtedly, all this is both insightful and existentially relevant. The connected notions of the open future and of a reality still in the making also turn the universe into a less claustrophobic place in which to live. Hope and passionate engagement are not absurd if the course of things is not predetermined, but can be oriented one way or another. Still, Whitehead does at times provide descriptions of God that make one seriously wonder whether the proposed theology can offer the sort of existential inspiration not solely religious people, but most thoughtful persons crave for. The following passage is particularly troublesome:

> The primordial appetitions that jointly constitute God's purpose are seeking intensity, and not preservation. Because they are primordial, there is nothing to preserve. *He, in his primordial nature, is unmoved by love for this particular, or that particular*; for in this foundational process of creativity, there are no preconstituted particulars. In the foundations of his being, God is indifferent alike to preservation and to novelty. He cares not whether an immediate occasion be old or new, so far as concerns derivation from its ancestry. His aim for it is depth of satisfaction as *an intermediate step towards the fulfillment of his own being*. (PR 105; my emphasis)

Apparently, in presenting to each single actuality a Form for realisation, God is not aiming at what is 'best' for the actuality; his aim is to turn the world into as beautiful an object as possible, so that his subsequent appropriation may provide him with a most intense experience. Furthermore, in suggesting ideals for realisation to the concrescing occasions, God is not moved by any moral impulse, but by aesthetic considerations. Worldly occasions too are advised to strive for the maximum of intensity in their experiences, in this sense, to become as 'God-like' as they can. This is a strange view indeed, as there is no intrinsic connection between the notions of 'depth of satisfaction' and 'morally right'; on the contrary, intensity of experience may even be achieved in immoral ways. Finally, this whole conception would seem to presuppose a quite idiosyncratic version of the old-fashioned idea of a great chain of being. Is Whitehead suggesting that individuals capable of a higher depth of intensity in their experiences are to be regarded as being closer to God than all others? This is, again, a somewhat dangerous view, as one fails to see why on this basis the life, say, of an artist (or, for that matter, of a creative philosopher) should not be regarded as ontologically higher (and not merely as more enjoyable) than the life of a person engaged in a more humble occupation.

All in all, from the point of view of a suffering human being, this conception of God is hardly likely to appear better than Aristotle's notion of a self-loving Deity. There is nothing here that justifies thinking of Whitehead's God as a caring, loving father.

Nor does Whitehead deal better than his predecessors with the problem of evil. His God cannot be charged with having any direct responsibility for its occurring, for he is not the world's Creator. It is also intellectually liberating to see that Whitehead makes no attempt to explain evil away by declaring it unreal. On the contrary, he apparently thinks that it is impossible to eradicate it from the world's history. He writes in one of his darker moods that 'life is robbery' and does not hesitate to condemn Leibniz for his claim that we live in the best of all possible worlds. As he explains:

> The Leibnizian theory of the 'best of possible worlds' is
> an audacious fudge produced in order to save the face of
> a Creator constructed by contemporary, and antecedent,
> theologians. (PR 47)

Nevertheless, the indifference of Whitehead's own God to our present and forthcoming sufferings does not make him truly worthy of any great admiration. God may indeed 'save' us in his consequent nature; by then, however, catastrophes of all sorts may have already occurred.

Existentially, this doctrine of God's consequent nature is an attempt to find an acceptable compromise between the deepest desires of the heart and what we experience as God's scandalous absence in the most tragic circumstances of our lives. But how convincing is it? There is no need to enter into details, as anyone can see that, to the millions of innocent victims of history, Whitehead's theory of a primarily egoistic God who saves us when all things have already taken place would appear as morally repulsive as Leibniz's theory of the best of all possible worlds. Whitehead underestimates the difficulty of his own conception when he says that God 'is a little oblivious as to morals' (PR 343).[4]

HOW COHERENT IS WHITEHEAD'S PROCESS VIEW OF NATURE?

One notable feature of Whitehead's dipolar conception is that it provides a basis for conceiving of the relationship between God and the world in a truly novel way. Traditionally God has either been identified with the world or conceived as a transcendent entity that could exist without it. In Whitehead's process theory, God and the world are neither wholly divorced from one another nor straightforwardly identified. The world needs God, as the worldly actualities receive their lure towards novelty from a grasp of the Forms existing within his primordial nature; God, on the other hand, needs the world, which he absorbs in his consequent nature. At every step of their development, the two sustain and modify each other, essentially contributing to the identity of the other without determining it. As Whitehead has it: 'The notion of God . . . is that of an actual entity immanent in the actual world, but transcending any finite cosmic epoch – a being at once actual, eternal, immanent, and transcendent' (PR 93).

There is, from a purely theoretical point of view, a certain beauty and elegance in this conception. But this new theological model does not come without some major technical difficulties. 'The presumption that there is only one genus of actual entities,' Whitehead writes, 'constitutes an ideal of cosmological theory to which the philosophy of organism endeavours to conform' (PR 110). In order to respect the requirement, it would now seem that even God should have to be conceived of as a series of occasions. But Whitehead denies this to be the case. If God were to reach satisfaction, the element of transcendence with respect to the world would be totally lost, as God would then become an objective constituent of the physical flux. Hence, we find Whitehead identifying God with a process of concrescence, one that never reaches satisfaction (PR 31). God can indeed be said to be an actual *entity*, yet not an actual *occasion*: 'The term "actual occasion" will always exclude God from its scope' (PR 88). One may well ask here whether this peculiarity should not be regarded as a violation of the requirement of ontological uniformity. To deny that God ever achieves satisfaction, moreover, is to say that he never becomes anything determinate. This makes it look doubtful whether he can be regarded as fully real after all; in a way, Whitehead postulates an ontological deficiency in God, which is a strange view to hold. Lastly, if God is not fully real, then it is difficult to see how he could be prehended by the worldly actualities, which is required if new Forms are to enter the cosmic process. All things considered, it does not seem true that '[i]n the philosophy of organism . . . God's existence is not generally different from that of other actual entities' (PR 75).

That Whitehead should have failed to provide a wholly satisfactory account of God's relationship to the world was only to be expected, as the task is an enormously difficult one. Whitehead's philosophical theology, moreover, is the less worked out part of his system. In passages that make one immediately realise what Russell meant when he said that 'something of the vicarage atmosphere always remained' (PM 95) in Whitehead's ways of feeling, God is more lyrically celebrated than analytically explained in such works as *Process and Reality* and *Religion in the Making* (1926). Still, Whitehead's main theological doctrines are deeply perplexing. There is a dark side to Whitehead's God that his admirers usually fail to acknowledge squarely. The notion of a Cosmic Intellect participating in the course of history also entails a rejection of the key ideas of emergence and self-organisation upon which his social theory of nature was based, in favour of an updated conception of providence and a modified form of creationism: can a Darwinian truly believe, as Whitehead does, in eternal metaphysical types?

As a matter of fact, the introduction of God determines not solely a change of doctrine, but of intellectual climate in Whitehead's entire philosophy as well. This momentous shift will be explored further in the next, conclusive chapter.

NOTES

1. Matt Ridley's *The Origin of Virtue: Human Instincts and the Evolution of Cooperation*, London and New York: Penguin, 1996, for instance, is an impressive attempt to explain the origin of altruistic behaviour in an evolutionary universe as well as to identify the ideal conditions under which such behaviour could flourish.
2. A. C. Ewing, *Idealism: A Critical Survey*, London: Methuen, 1934, p. 412.

3. A slightly different version of this objection is raised by T. L. S. Sprigge against Hartshorne's Whiteheadian conception of God in *The God of Metaphysics*, Oxford: Clarendon Press, 2006, p. 450.
4. Among interpreters sympathetic to Whitehead's philosophy, few have been willing to face these difficulties in his conception of God. One exception is Sprigge, *The God of Metaphysics*, pp. 454–8. The charge of 'elitism' is raised by John Hick, *Philosophy of Religion*, Englewood Cliffs, NJ: Prentice Hall, 1990, pp. 52–5.

CHAPTER 8

Conclusion: The Ethics of Creativity – A Deweyan Critique

RECONSTRUCTING PHILOSOPHY

Whitehead believed that philosophy had lost its force in the contemporary world. Instead of being a progressive factor in human culture, it had become a sterile, self-enclosed academic exercise with no relevance to the most concrete problems of humankind. This was evidenced by philosophers' increasing love of polemics. His disenchanted view about the status of the discipline can be gathered from a famous passage in *Adventures of Ideas*, where he says that philosophy 'is not – or, at least, should not be – a ferocious debate between irritable professors' (AI 98).

The way to make philosophy relevant to human life is to rehabilitate speculative metaphysics. Metaphysics tells us the way that all things hang together and the place we occupy in the overall scheme of things. It gives an answer to the question 'What does it all come to?' (PR xiii). Functioning like a secularised religion, it provides a framework that human beings can appeal to when they are uncertain about what direction their lives must take. The problem of vindicating speculative metaphysics as an enterprise 'productive of important knowledge' (PR 3) has a social dimension as well, for civilisation cannot subsist in a metaphysical vacuum. In the absence of an inspiring metaphysical vision, Whitehead argues in *Adventures of Ideas*, humankind cannot avoid falling into barbarism. One has to prevent the crisis of philosophy, which Whitehead interprets as a crisis of creativity, from becoming a crisis of civilisation (AI 99).

It is with respect to the double problem of infusing new life into philosophy and making it relevant to our private and social lives that we find a major point of contact between Whitehead and one of the leading intellectual figures of his day, John Dewey. According to Dewey, philosophy had been too long concerned with merely 'dialectical' (by which he meant unreal, artificial) questions. Moreover, he too believed that this impasse was a danger for civilisation: 'contemporary society, the world over,' he wrote, 'is in need of more general and fundamental enlightenment and guidance than it now possesses' (RIP 124).

As a matter of fact, Whitehead thought he had found in Dewey a philosophical ally. In *Process and Reality* he explicitly says that his book is an attempt to continue a line of thought inaugurated by, among others, James and Dewey (PR xiii). In a paper of 1939 titled 'John Dewey and his Influence', Whitehead praises the American pragmatist as one of those men 'who have made philosophic thought relevant to the needs of their own day' (ESP 91). Dewey, too, appreciated Whitehead's philosophy, but he also criticised him bitterly for what he believed to be his half-way rejection of traditional conceptions of philosophy. Specifically, in 'The Philosophy of Whitehead' (a paper published in 1941 when both thinkers had reached maturity, for Dewey was 82 years old at the time, Whitehead 80), Dewey complained that Whitehead had converted 'moral idealism, the idealism of action, into ontological idealism' (PW 661), a conversion he took to be the fatal mistake of all Western metaphysics.

The meaning of this charge is not immediately obvious and some significant (hence also debatable) interpretative work is needed to make it fully explicit. In order to understand it, one has first to appreciate the standpoint from which it is made. This requires getting some acquaintance with Dewey's overall philosophical project of reconstructing philosophy.

PHILOSOPHERS' LOVE OF ORDER

Dewey was an immensely prolific author, but the essentials of his critique of traditional ways of thought can be easily gathered from his philosophical manifesto, *Reconstruction in Philosophy* (1920), as well as from two acknowledged masterpieces, *Experience and Nature* (1925) and *The Quest for Certainty* (1929). In these books, Dewey presents a critique of classical metaphysics that pivots upon two main ideas.

First, Dewey argues, classical metaphysics represents the world as having an already accomplished structure, hence in the end as not capable of change. Classical metaphysics takes the world to be fixed and necessarily perfect. Secondly, the metaphysician traditionally claims to have achieved a secure grasp of this structure, so secure, indeed, that it cannot be cast into doubt by any later arguments or subsequent philosophies. Hence, each metaphysician makes a claim to finality or certainty. Not surprisingly, Dewey observes, metaphysicians typically love axioms rather than experiments – a point Whitehead would have endorsed. Given the amount of conflict and frustration we experience in our daily lives, the idea that the world in which we live is a perfect one should strike any thinking person as entirely absurd. This naively optimistic view was nevertheless able to captivate outstanding and highly sophisticated intellects such as those of Plato, Aristotle and Leibniz. As Dewey tries to show in a series of impressive historical surveys, the doctrine of the rationality of the real dominated the philosophical imagination of the Western world, not just Hegel's.

In order to understand this perplexing fact, Dewey begins to look at philosophy with the eyes of the anthropologist. We have to consider what basic human needs philosophy is called upon to satisfy, the needs that generate it in the first place, rather than the logical content of its doctrines. While the world in which we live is a dangerous place, the metaphysical systems of the past tell us that – at a deeper level – reality is harmonious. The conflicts and imperfections of ordinary life exist only *sub specie temporis*; viewed *sub specie aeternitatis*, they are 'unreal'. By propagating this view, metaphysical systems have been able to work as sedatives for our deepest fears; this explains why they have been believed in the past. In the long run, however, a philosophy of consolation is bound to be a conservative rather than a progressive force in human life and culture. The belief that all is well and that the world has an immutable structure deprives us of any desire to change it – it makes us passive spectators rather than active agents.

As this brief account of Dewey's critique of metaphysics makes clear, he does not try to liberate us from its spell by way of direct logical argumentation. A more effective way to liberate our minds from dangerous – not because false, but because disempowering – ideas is by reconstructing the genesis of our beliefs. The epistemic model for this kind of philosophical criticism is not empirical science, but psychoanalysis. Philosophical criticism works like a therapy in which the patient is expected to experience a reawakening of sorts – recognising at once the folly of his or her previous beliefs and ways of conduct. Needless to say, this way of practising philosophical criticism runs against the entire academic praxis, which privileges logical over historical analysis, rational arguments over human motives. From Dewey's perspective, this simply shows the emptiness of much academic philosophy, which fails to pay sufficient attention to the concrete conditions under which human thoughts originate and flourish. After all, philosophy is itself a form of 'experience' – in Dewey's jargon, the outcome of a human's interactions with a sometimes supportive, sometimes indifferent, but most frequently hostile natural environment.

THE TASK OF PHILOSOPHY

It follows from Dewey's analysis that philosophy must either be reconstructed or perish altogether. The new conception of philosophy that emerges from his writings is that of philosophy as a socially oriented enterprise – philosophy as cultural criticism. As Dewey views things, the philosopher's task is that of bringing to the fore the unconscious conceptual presuppositions of his or her age, showing their origin in human experience and history. At the same time, Dewey believes in experimental testing as the sole way of establishing what can justifiably be asserted. Thus, the philosopher must ask the community in which he or she lives to evaluate the identified presuppositions by submitting them to the judgement of experience. In this way, the philosopher comes to perform an important social role; if the investigations are successful, they will be able to open new conceptual spaces. The role envisaged by Dewey for the philosopher is not that of an Aristotelian knower of (ultimate, incorrigible) Truth, but the Promethean role of a cultural liberator. The philosopher frees us from those invisible mental prisons in which we think – and live.

What does this mean in terms of actual praxis? Should the philosopher be a teacher, a journalist, a writer of books? Should he or she appear on television or make his or her voice heard on the radio? I take it to be an essential part of Dewey's liberal outlook that it is impossible to spell out in advance what precise form a critique of culture must take. There may be more than one way to be a cultural critic. One simply has to pick up – or invent – his or her own way of performing the job and communicating its results to contemporaries.

Before Dewey, an essayist and popular lecturer like Ralph Waldo Emerson might have been this kind of philosopher. Today, Stanley Cavell or Cornell West could be seen as its exemplification. (Process philosophers like John Cobb and David Ray Griffin could also be included in this group of socially responsible thinkers.) Of course, a neo-pragmatist like Richard Rorty is in many ways a quintessentially Deweyan figure. But one must be aware that Dewey would not have accepted Rorty's basic assumption that 'there is nothing outside language to which language attempts to become adequate'.[1] Dewey notoriously criticises what he terms 'the spectator-theory of knowledge' – the view that knowledge is essentially a matter of grasping or passively reproducing within the mirror of one's own mind the basic structure of external reality. Nevertheless, he does not go so far as to deny the relevance of the external world to our knowledge-claims. As just noted, Dewey argues that any new language-game or conceptual scheme must be tested against the bedrock of experience. This means that – like Whitehead and the other great pragmatists, Peirce and James – Dewey is a realist of sorts who believes experience to embody a non-conceptual, extralinguistic criterion capable of establishing what can – and what cannot – be legitimately asserted.

HOW MANY WHITEHEADS?

We are now in a position to attempt an interpretation of Dewey's laconic claim that Whitehead has converted 'moral idealism, the idealism of action, into ontological idealism' (PW 661). Dewey recognises that Whitehead's philosophy introduces many revolutionary novelties. He explicitly praises some of Whitehead's ideas, such as his organic view of human beings, his enlarged conception of experience as including more than sense-experience, the idea of continuity between humans and nature, his phenomenological analysis of a moment of human mentality, his account of the subject/object distinction (PW 645–56). Dewey also defends Whitehead's writings from the common critique that they are too obscure. Since Whitehead is trying to articulate new philosophical categories, what else could he do but develop a new philosophical terminology (PW 660)?

Interestingly, Dewey also acknowledges that Whitehead, at times, exemplifies that new kind of progressive intellectual he has in mind, especially in *Science and the Modern World* and *Adventures of Ideas*. As Dewey has it, Whitehead has come closer than most philosophers to 'stating the nature of the region from which he sets out' (PW 644) – that is, he has gone a long way towards making explicit the unrecognised presuppositions that govern modern philosophical thinking. Unfortunately, Dewey would seem to contend, there is another – conservative – side to Whitehead's philosophy.

In the already mentioned 'The Philosophy of Whitehead', Dewey praises Whitehead for his ability to disclose new horizons to the human imagination:

> Of one thing I am quite sure. He has opened an immensely fruitful new path for subsequent philosophy to follow . . . The result is an almost incomparable suggestiveness on all sorts of topics – in case a mind is not closed to suggestion from a new source. (PW 659)

Then he makes a more sceptical comment:

> But I am not sure that he does not frequently block and divert his own movements on the road he is opening by subjecting his conclusions to a combination of considerations too exclusively derived from a combination of mathematics with excessive piety toward those historic philosophers from whom he has derived valuable suggestions. (PW 659)

Dewey substantiates his thesis that there are two Whiteheads – a good one who liberates human creativity and a bad one who inhibits it – by referring to Whitehead's definition of speculative metaphysics. As Whitehead says in *Process and Reality*, speculative metaphysics is an attempt to frame 'a coherent, logical, necessary system of general ideas in terms of which every element of our experience can be interpreted' (PR 3). According to Dewey, the conception of philosophy that emerges from this passage suffices to classify Whitehead as a philosopher of the 'classic' stripe:

This [Whitehead's] conception of the nature and office of
philosophy is in line with the classic tradition, according to
which philosophy is that branch of theory which tells, in the
theoretical form appropriate to knowledge as knowledge, the
story of the ultimate metaphysical or ontological structure of
the universe. (PW 657)

Dewey even charges Whitehead with making essences ontologically prior over actual, individual things:

Assignment of ontological priority to general characters and
essences, and subordination to them of the existences actually
observed in nature accords, to all appearances, not simply with
the Platonic point of view, but with the assimilation of the
proper subject-matter of philosophy (the constitution of nature)
to that of mathematical theory. (PW 657–8)

In these passages, Dewey depicts Whitehead as a full-fledged Platonist who believes the world to have a rational structure. Given his critique of traditional conceptions of metaphysics, however, the real import of this charge would seem to be that Whitehead's metaphysics is as much in danger of making us morally inept as the systems of the past. On this interpretation, to say that Whitehead has converted 'the idealism of action' into 'ontological idealism' is to say that, like all systems of the past, Whitehead's metaphysics inhibits our moral and intellectual energies rather than releasing them, although admittedly this is not a thesis Dewey states in such explicit, radical terms.

What is to be made of this charge, provided it really is Dewey's own? This would certainly be a strong accusation against a philosophy like Whitehead's that aims at being relevant to human life. However, as a matter of fact, it seems to involve a series of grave misunderstandings. In the first place, the ideal of a coherent system is, for Whitehead, nothing more than this – an ideal of reason. It belongs to the nature of reason to search for systematic connections. Nowhere does Whitehead assume that full rationality is already realised in actual existence; on the contrary, he stresses the fact that the world is a mixture of chaos and order, contingency and necessity – there is indeed regularity, but it is not ubiquitous. Secondly, as noted above, the speculative scheme is not put forward in a dogmatic spirit. Its nature is that of a hypothesis. Whitehead has abandoned what Dewey sees as the Cartesian quest for certainty typical of all modern philosophy. As he has it: 'In philosophical discussion, the merest hint of dogmatic certainty as to finality of statement is an exhibition of folly' (PR xiv). Thirdly, essences (in Whitehead's terminology, 'eternal objects') are far from being granted ontological priority over individual actualities. On the contrary, without some actuality that exemplifies them, they would be nothing. Fourthly, if there is something Whitehead's philosophy leaves conceptual room for, it is precisely the possibility of change: future events are neither mechanically predetermined nor already in existence. As a matter of fact, Whitehead's universe is precisely that kind of process universe Dewey himself celebrates in *Experience and Nature*, 'a world which is not finished and which has not consistently made up its mind where it is going and what it is going to do' (EN 76).

Apparently, by locating Whitehead within the classic tradition, Dewey fails to grasp both the novelty of his conception of speculative metaphysics as well as some of his main doctrines. Surprisingly enough, Dewey himself seems to have more than just a dim awareness of this, as at one point he writes: 'Deficiency of my own intellectual grasp may be the cause of my belief that this entire strain of thought [Whitehead's] substitutes abstract logical connectedness for the concrete existential temporal connectedness' (PW 658). He even comes to the point of confessing: 'I wonder whether I am on the right track when I make that interpretation' (PW 658).

An uneasiness produced in an honest mind by the suspicion that he is doing injustice to another philosopher's thought might be the reason why Dewey concludes his paper with the following, laudatory words:

> It is doubtless true, as Mr. Whitehead has said, that the reaction against dogmatic and imposed systematizations marking so many historic philosophies, has led other thinkers to undue neglect of the kind of system that is important. But the abstract formalization that defines systematization upon the model provided by mathematics does not shut out the possibility of that kind of system in which what is known about Nature, physical and human, is brought to bear upon

intelligent criticism of what exists . . . and upon construction of alternatives, of possibilities, which the play of free critical intelligence indicates to be better worth while. The substance of Whitehead's system I find to be of the latter sort; its formal statements seem to me often to lean in the former direction. (PW 661)

This passage runs counter to the whole drift of Dewey's critique of Whitehead. This final praise of the 'substance' of Whitehead's philosophy as consisting in his ability to promote the free play of the critical imagination is hardly consistent with the previous charge of having converted the 'idealism of action' into 'ontological idealism'.

DEWEY'S DEEPER UNDERSTANDING

In spite of all this, it would be wrong to reject Dewey's critique as entirely mistaken. This becomes clear if one compares Dewey's and Whitehead's respective epistemologies of value: how do we know what we ought to do? As Dewey explains in a chapter of *Reconstruction in Philosophy* entitled 'Reconstruction in Moral Conceptions', we know moral concepts the way we know anything else – by way of experiment and reflection upon past experiences. We have to mobilise our creative powers, for values are not found, but constructed. We project our ends upon an uncertain future – and experience teaches us whether they were really worth pursuing or not.

This is an extension of the experimental method of science to the ethical field. As Dewey reconstructs it in his *Logic: The Theory of Inquiry* (1938), the method involves five main steps: (1) an inchoate uneasiness is felt by the inquiring subject; (2) the inquirer tries to translate the uneasiness into a clearly formulated problem; (3) a hypothesis about the right way of conduct is imaginatively elaborated; (4) the hypothesis is analysed with regard to its potential capability of solving the problem at issue; (5) eventually, the hypothesis is empirically tested. According to Dewey, this method should be applied not solely at the individual, but also at the social level. What ends a society must strive for are matters to be decided by way of imagination (which is required to formulate the problem and the possible solutions to it) and experiment.

Dewey sees himself here as making a revolutionary move. Taking this stance requires abandoning the long-cherished notion that there is an uncontestable source of values. As he explains,

> Ethical theory began among the Greeks as an attempt to find a regulation for the conduct of life which should have a rational basis and purpose instead of being derived from custom. But reason as a substitute for custom was under the obligation of supplying objects and laws as fixed as those of custom had been. (RIP 161)

This idea, he goes on to say, took many forms in the history of philosophy:

> Some have held that the end is loyalty or obedience to a higher power or authority; and they have variously found this higher principle in Divine Will, the will of the secular ruler, the maintenance of institutions in which the purpose of superiors is embodied, and the rational consciousness of duty. (RIP 161)

The idea that Dewey is here condemning as conservative now resurfaces in Whitehead's philosophy. Whitehead identifies the realm of values with that select portion of the realm of eternal objects that God has judged to be worthy of realisation. According to his teleological account of the process of concrescence, each novel occasion of experience is lured by an ideal presented by God as an end worth pursuing: 'God is the principle of concretion; namely, he is that actual entity from which each temporal concrescence receives that initial aim from which its self-causation starts' (PR 244). When the notion of an initial aim provided by God is considered in respect of its existential import or overall human significance, it seems only straightforward to conclude that Whitehead is urging us to look within our consciences in order to enjoy the benefit of a private divine revelation. Our first obligation is to become aware of what God wants us to become; we are asked to take the attitude of silent listeners, not that of creative subjects.

To see this is to see what Whitehead means when he characterises religion as 'the art and the theory of the internal life of man, so far as it depends on the man himself and on what is permanent in the nature of things' (RM 16) or, alternatively and more forcefully, as 'what the individual does with his own solitariness' (RM 16). But it is also to see that Whitehead is far from having abandoned the traditional – and for Dewey reactionary – notion that morality involves 'loyalty or obedience to a higher power or authority' (RIP 161). It would be beside the point to object that Whitehead's God does not violently oblige finite individuals to follow his decrees or threaten them with the atrocities of hell if they do not, but rather operates like a caring parent, slowly and patiently by way of persuasion. This true and important remark does not alter the fact that, as far as morals are concerned, Whitehead makes inner authority superior to the deliverances of experience. What turns a possible form of definiteness or eternal object into a valuable end is simply the fact that it is so valued by God. Later experience can do nothing to reverse this appraisal – we may fail to respond adequately to the divine call, but God cannot be shown to have been wrong.

Certainly, an epistemology of internal private revelation does not square well with Whitehead's experimentalist outlook. And indeed, what else is this particular theory of Whitehead if not a return to those a priori or intuitionist modes of thought he is so critical of in other parts of his philosophy?

CONCLUSION: AN AMBIGUOUS ADVENTURE

In *Process and Reality* Whitehead argues that the (partial) order of the physical world indicates the existence of an ordering, directing mind:

> Apart from the intervention of God, there could be nothing new in the world, and no order in the world. The course of creation would be a dead level of ineffectiveness, with all balance and intensity progressively excluded by the cross currents of incompatibility. (PR 247)

One can only admire the audacity involved in the attempt at integrating the teleological argument within an evolutionary metaphysics. 'Today, in an age of democracy,' Whitehead furthermore remarks while commenting on Plato's idea that philosophers shall be kings, 'the kings are the plain citizens' (AI 98). But one cannot avoid also wondering whether the very notion that order necessarily degenerates into chaos in the absence of a dominating *archê* is really compatible with a sincere commitment to the values of a democratic community.

Equally perplexing is Whitehead's claim that there could be nothing new in the world apart from God. As becomes clear in a passage in which he criticises Hume's theory of the imagination, this is meant to apply to our concepts as well. The imagination may reorganise our ideas into novel combinatorial forms, Whitehead argues, but where does that new form come from? If the mind derives it from previous experiences, then the new idea produced by the imagination is true only in an impoverished sense of the word; radical novelty requires a different kind of source:

> Hume admits that there are novel compound ideas which are not copies of compound impressions. Thus he should also admit that there is a novel simple idea conveying the novel 'manner' [of combination], which is not a copy of an impression. (PR 132)

In *Science and the Modern World*, Whitehead also observes that 'Pythagoras in founding European philosophy and European mathematics, endowed them with the luckiest of lucky guesses'. Then he cryptically asks: 'or, was it a flash of divine genius, penetrating to the inmost nature of things?' (SMW 37). As remarked in Chapter 2, Peirce had explained the wonder of abduction by means of a theory of cosmic attunement; Whitehead's statements now suggest a theory of divine inspiration. At this point, one begins to wonder: what remains of human creativity, if we have to rely upon the whispering of a larger mind in order to conceive of any new idea?

All in all, what in this chapter has been (rightly or wrongly) identified as Dewey's critique is wrong as far as details are concerned, but correct with regard to its general import; there are anti-Whiteheadian tendencies in Whitehead's philosophy. Consider, to conclude with, the following passage from *Adventures of Ideas*:

> Mankind is now in one of its rare moods of shifting its outlook. The mere compulsion of tradition has lost its force. It is our business – philosophers, students, and practical men – to re-create and reenact a vision of the world, including those elements of reverence and order without which society lapses into riot, and penetrated through and through with unflinching rationality. Such a vision is the knowledge which Plato identified with virtue. (AI 99)

Whitehead is more liberal than Plato in the *Republic*, since he admits 'practical men', and not solely philosophers, to the vision of the Good. Still, our duty is not to question, but to obediently realise the envisioned ideal order. Otherwise disaster will ensue. But it is not clear why we should be obedient, given Whitehead's view that God aims at the heightening of intensity of his own experience. Nor is it obvious that submission to the wishes of an egoistic God has anything to do with 'virtue'.

As Dewey saw, Whitehead's speculative journey is a fascinating yet ambiguous adventure, always suspended between insight and delusion, radical innovation and adherence to old-fashioned ideas, the celebration of critical thinking and the need for an unquestionable authority. His philosophy escapes any easy judgement: it belongs to a progressive future as much as it does to a conservative, perhaps even slightly reactionary, past.

NOTES

1. Richard Rorty, *Philosophy as Cultural Politics: Philosophical Papers*, Vol. 4, Cambridge: Cambridge University Press, 2007, p. 109.

Appendix: The Making of a Metaphysician – A Biographical Note

Alfred North Whitehead was born on 15 February 1861 at Ramsgate on the Isle of Thanet in Kent, the son of a schoolmaster and clergyman. At the age of 14 he was sent to Sherborne public school in Dorset, which had recently gained an outstanding reputation. Here he acquired a solid knowledge of Latin and Greek: 'I can still feel the dullness of Xenophon, Sallust, and Livy' (ESP 9) was his confession towards the end of his life.

In 1880 he entered Cambridge University with a scholarship in mathematics. Whatever instruction he had in philosophy (history and theology were his other true passions) was obtained independently, by means of solitary lectures and discussions with friends and colleagues. The invitation to join the legendary debating club known as the 'Apostles' gave him ample opportunities to reflect upon philosophical issues and to exercise his dialectical skill. Life in Cambridge during these years, Whitehead would later recall, had 'the appearance of a daily Platonic dialogue' (ESP 10).

Upon the completion of his studies, Whitehead was appointed a fellow of Trinity College on the basis of a now lost dissertation on James Clerk Maxwell's *Treatise on Electricity and Magnetism* in 1884. He taught mathematics and mathematical physics at Cambridge until 1910. This was a golden age for the university, witnessing the rise of analytic philosophy in the works of George Edward Moore and Whitehead's own pupil, Bertrand Russell. The outstanding James Ward (now almost totally forgotten), John Ellis McTaggart and Charles Dunbar Broad were among his colleagues.

While in Cambridge, Whitehead published *On Mathematical Concepts of the Material World* (1906) and *The Axioms of Projective Geometry* (1907). His most important contribution to philosophy during these years was the logical treatise he co-authored with Bertrand Russell, the monumental *Principia Mathematica* (1910–13) – 'a big book no part of which is wholly due to either' (PM 93), as Russell generously acknowledged.

In 1914 Whitehead became Professor of Applied Mathematics at the Imperial College of Science and Technology in London, where he had moved a few years earlier. While in London he regularly attended meetings of the newly founded Aristotelian Society, which gave him plenty of opportunities to continue his informal education in philosophy. Whitehead's main works from this period are *An Enquiry Concerning the Principles of Natural Knowledge* (1919), *The Concept of Nature* (1920) and *The Principle of Relativity* (1922). One can see him here already moving towards his final system, as he advocates an ontology of interrelated, 'overlapping' events. A collection of miscellaneous educational writings, *The Organization of Thought, Educational and Scientific* (1917), was also published during this period.

At the age of 63 Whitehead enthusiastically accepted an invitation to teach philosophy at Harvard, Massachusetts. This was the birthplace of pragmatism, the university which until only a few years earlier had been home to Charles Sanders Peirce, William James, Josiah Royce and George Santayana. 'For many generations,' Whitehead wrote, 'the North American Continent will be the living centre of human civilization. Thought and action will derive from it, and refer to it' (ESP 91). On American soil, he found an atmosphere favourable to the kind of revisionary thinking he was about to develop; it is here that he eventually flourished as a metaphysician.

The core of his metaphysical view is articulated in the trilogy (as he himself called it) that consists of *Science and the Modern World* (1925), *Adventures of Ideas* (1933) and the systematic *Process and Reality* (1929). This book was originally delivered as a series of Gifford Lectures in Edinburgh in the years 1927 and 1928, the invitation itself constituting a clear sign of the esteem in which he was held by his contemporaries.

But the lectures turned out to be a failure. This is hardly surprising, since *Process and Reality* is not a book for the general public: 'In these lectures,' Whitehead writes in its Preface, 'I have endeavoured to compress the material derived from years of meditation' (PR xiv).

Whitehead's other metaphysical works from this period include *Religion in the Making* (1926), *Symbolism: Its Meaning and Effect* (1927), *The Function of Reason* (1929) and the later *Modes of Thought* (1938). These shorter books deal in an experimental fashion with specific points in the system. They are written in an engaging style, and vividly communicate the spirit of adventure that permeates his thought.

Whitehead's last philosophical writings include two lectures bearing the very Platonic titles 'Mathematics and the Good' (given at Harvard in 1939) and 'Immortality' (given at the Harvard Divinity School in 1941). A collection of essays on various philosophical subjects, *Essays in Science and Philosophy*, was published in 1948, shortly after his death on 30 December 1947. This book also includes four brief autobiographical papers: 'The Education of a Gentleman' (1926), 'England and the Narrow Seas' (1927), 'Memories' (1936) and 'Autobiographical Notes' (1941).

Unexpectedly, in these autobiographical essays Whitehead reveals little or nothing about his own life struggles and inner torments. His subject is never himself, but the community in which he grew up as a small boy and the larger historical happenings that shaped its peculiar atmosphere. What he depicts are that world's unique inhabitants, their lost ways of living, thinking and feeling.

Whitehead also likes to give detailed descriptions of the almost magical landscape in which he spent his infancy and early youth. One typical passage reads as follows:

> But closer to my home, within the Island or just beyond its borders, English history had left every type of relic. There stood the great walls of Richborough Castle built by the Romans, and the shores of Ebbes Fleet where the Saxons and Augustine landed. A mile or so inland was the village of Minster with its wonderful Abbey Church, retaining some touches of Roman stone-work, but dominated by its glorious Norman architecture. On this spot Augustine preached his first sermon. (ESP 8)

This passage is, among other things, a splendid illustration of a philosophical idea. We are not isolated 'histories', but exist within an ongoing history, itself made up by innumerable events, shaped by notable personalities and permeated with strong emotional values. The world is a process made up of processes, one of which is our own life; the past is gone, yet it is still affecting us.

These are the central insights around which Whitehead's philosophy is woven, and his autobiographical pieces, veritable instances of 'applied metaphysics', communicate them in an extremely simple and concrete fashion.

Bibliography

Backer, G., and K. J. Morris, *Descartes' Dualism*, London and New York: Routledge, 1996.

Basile, P., 'It Must Be True – But How Can it Be? Some Remarks on Panpsychism and Mental Composition', in P. Basile et al. (eds), *The Metaphysics of Consciousness*, Cambridge: Cambridge University Press, 2010, pp. 93–112.

— 'Learning from Leibniz: Whitehead (and Russell) on Minds, Matter, and Monads', *British Journal for the History of Philosophy* 23/6, 2015, pp. 1128–49.

— *Leibniz, Whitehead and the Metaphysics of Causation*, Basingstoke and New York: Palgrave Macmillan, 2009.

— 'Materialist vs. Panexperientialist Physicalism: Where Do We Stand?', *Process Studies* 39/2, 2010, pp. 264–84.

— 'Overcoming the Legacy of Modern Thought: Whitehead's Revisionary Metaphysics of Mind and Nature', in W. Seager (ed.), *Routledge Handbook of Panpsychism*, London and New York: Routledge, forthcoming 2017.

— 'Russell on Spinoza's Substance Monism', *Metaphysica: International Journal for Ontology and Metaphysics* 13/1, 2012, pp. 27–41.

— 'Self and World: the Radical Empiricism of Hume, Bradley and James', *Bradley Studies* 9/2, 2003, pp. 93–100.

Basile, P., J. Kiverstein and P. Phemister (eds), *The Metaphysics of Consciousness*, Cambridge: Cambridge University Press, 2010.

Basile, P., and L. McHenry (eds), *Consciousness, Reality and Value: Essays in Honour of T. L. S. Sprigge*, Frankfurt: Ontos Verlag, 2007.

Brown, S., 'The Professionalization of British Philosophy', in W. Mander (ed.), *The Oxford Handbook of British Philosophy in the Nineteenth Century*, Oxford: Oxford University Press, 2014, pp. 619–40.

Chalmers, D., *The Conscious Mind: In Search of a Fundamental Theory*, Oxford: Oxford University Press, 1996.

Christian, W., *An Interpretation of Whitehead's Metaphysics*, New Haven, CT: Yale University Press, 1959.

Clayton, P., *Mind and Emergence*, Oxford: Oxford University Press, 2006.

Cobb, J., and D. R. Griffin (eds), *Mind and Nature: Essays on the Interface of Science and Philosophy*, Washington, DC: University Press of America, 1977.

Della Rocca, M., *Spinoza*, London and New York: Routledge, 2008.

Dewey, J., *Experience and Nature* [1925], New York: Dover, 1958.

— *Logic: The Theory of Inquiry*, New York: Henry Holt, 1938.

— 'The Philosophy of Whitehead', in P. A. Schilpp (ed.), *The Philosophy of Alfred North Whitehead*, La Salle, IL: Open Court, 1941, pp. 641–61.

— *The Quest for Certainty*, New York: Minton, Balch and Co., 1929.

— *Reconstruction in Philosophy* [1920], Boston: Beacon Press, 1948.

Di Poppa, F., 'Spinoza and Process Ontology', *The Southern Journal of Philosophy* 48/3, 2010, pp. 272–94

Emmett, D., *The Effectiveness of Causes*, Albany, NY: State University of New York Press, 1985.

— *Whitehead's Philosophy of Organism*, Westport, CT: Greenwood Press, 1966.

Ewing, A. C., *Idealism: A Critical Survey*, London: Methuen, 1934.

Ford, L., *The Emergence of Whitehead's Metaphysics: 1925–1929*, Albany, NY: State University of New York Press, 1984.

Ford, L., and G. L. Kline (eds), *Explorations in Whitehead's Philosophy*, New York: Fordham University Press, 1983.

Ford, M., *William James's Philosophy: A New Perspective*, Amherst, MA: University of Massachusetts Press, 1982.

Forrest, P., 'Sprigge's Spinoza', in P. Basile and L. McHenry (eds), *Consciousness, Reality and Value: Essays in Honour of T. L. S. Sprigge*, Frankfurt: Ontos Verlag, 2007.

Freeman, A. (ed.), *Consciousness and its Place in Nature*, Exeter: Imprint Academic, 2006.

Griffin, D. R., *Unsnarling the World-Knot: Consciousness, Freedom and the Mind–Body Problem*, Berkeley: University of California Press, 1998.

Haack, S., 'Descriptive and Revisionary Metaphysics', *Philosophical Studies* 35, 1979, pp. 361–71.

Hartshorne, C., *Creative Synthesis and Philosophic Method*, London: SCM Press, 1970.

— *Insights and Oversights of Great Thinkers*, Albany, NY: State University of New York Press, 1983.

— 'Physics and Psychics: The Place of Mind in Nature', in J. Cobb and D. R. Griffin (eds), *Mind and Nature*, Washington, DC: University Press of America, 1977, pp. 89–96.

— *Whitehead's Philosophy: Selected Essays*, Lincoln, NE, and London: University of Nebraska Press, 1972.

Hatfield, G., *Descartes and the Meditations*, New York: Routledge, 2003.

Hick, J., *Philosophy of Religion*, Englewood Cliffs, NJ: Prentice Hall, 1990.

Hocking, W. E., 'Whitehead as I Knew Him', in G. K. Kline (ed.), *Alfred North Whitehead: Essays on his Philosophy*, Englewood Cliffs, NJ: Prentice Hall, 1963, pp. 1–17.

Hosinsky, T. E., *Stubborn Fact and Creative Advance: An Introduction to the Metaphysics of Alfred North Whitehead*, New York: Rowman and Littlefield, 1993.

Hume, D., *A Treatise of Human Nature* [1739–40], ed. D. F. Norton and M. J. Norton, Oxford: Oxford University Press, 2000.

Ishiguro, H., 'Leibniz's Theory of the Ideality of Relations', in H. Frankfurt (ed.), *Leibniz: A Collection of Critical Essays*, New York: Anchor Books, 1972, pp. 191–224.

James, W., *Essays in Radical Empiricism*, New York: Longmans, Green, 1912.
— *The Principles of Psychology*, vol. I, New York: Dover, 1890.
Jones, J., *Intensity: An Essay in Whiteheadian Ontology*, Nashville, TN: Vanderbilt University Press, 1998.
Kim, J., *Mind in a Physical World: An Essay on the Mind–Body Problem and Mental Causation*, Cambridge, MA: MIT Press, 1998.
— 'The Mind–Body Problem at Century's Turn', in B. Leiter (ed.), *The Future for Philosophy*, Oxford: Clarendon Press, 2004.
Kraus, E. M., *The Metaphysics of Experience: A Companion to Whitehead's 'Process and Reality'*, New York: Fordham University Press, 1988.
Kuntz, P. G., *Alfred North Whitehead*, Boston: Twayne, 1984.
Ladyman, J., and D. Ross (with D. Spurrett and J. Collier), *Every Thing Must Go. Metaphysics Naturalized*, Oxford: Oxford University Press, 2007.
Lango, J., 'The Time of Whitehead's Concrescence', *Process Studies* 30/1, 2001, pp. 3–21.
— *Whitehead's Ontology*, Albany, NY: State University of New York Press, 1972.
Leclerc, I., *Whitehead's Metaphysics*, London: George Allen and Unwin, 1958.
Leibniz, G. W., *Philosophical Essays*, ed. and trans. R. Ariew and D. Garber, Indianapolis: Hackett, 1989.
Locke, J., *An Essay Concerning Human Understanding* [1689], ed. Peter H. Nidditch, Oxford: Oxford University Press, 1975.
Lowe, V., *Alfred North Whitehead: The Man and his Work*, 2 vols, Baltimore, MD, and London: Johns Hopkins University Press, 1985 and 1990.
Mander W., *British Idealism: A History*, Oxford: Oxford University Press, 2011.
Mander W. (ed.), *The Oxford Handbook of British Philosophy in the Nineteenth Century*, Oxford: Oxford University Press, 2014.
Mates, B., *The Philosophy of Leibniz: Metaphysics and Language*, Oxford and New York: Oxford University Press, 1986.

McGinn, C., *The Problem of Consciousness*, Oxford: Basil Blackwell, 1991.

Moravcsik, J., *Plato and Platonism*, Oxford: Blackwell, 1992.

Mugnai, M., *Leibniz's Theory of Relations*, Stuttgart: Meiner Verlag, 1992.

Nagel, T., *Mind and Cosmos: Why the Materialist Neo-Darwinian Conception of Nature is Almost Certainly False*, Oxford and New York: Oxford University Press, 2012.

— 'Panpsychism', in *Mortal Questions*, Cambridge: Cambridge University Press, 1979, pp. 181–95.

— *The View from Nowhere*, Oxford and New York: Oxford University Press, 1986.

Nobo, J. L., *Whitehead's Metaphysics of Extension and Solidarity*, Albany, NY: State University of New York Press, 1986.

Parkinson, G. H. R., *Logic and Reality in Leibniz's Metaphysics*, Oxford: Clarendon Press, 1965.

Passmore, J., *A Hundred Years of Philosophy*, London: Penguin, 1957.

Peirce, C. S., 'The Architecture of Theories', *The Monist*, 1891, pp. 161–76.

— 'Deduction, Induction and Hypothesis', *Popular Science Monthly* 13, 1878, pp. 470–82.

Phemister, P., *Leibniz and the Natural World. Activity, Passivity and Corporeal Substances in Leibniz's Philosophy*, Dordrecht: Springer, 2005.

Price, L., *Dialogues of Alfred North Whitehead*, London: Max Reinhardt, 1954.

Quine, W. v. O., 'Mr. Strawson on Logical Theory', *Mind* 62, 1953, pp. 433–51.

Rescher, N., 'Leibniz on Intermonadic Relations', in N. Rescher, *On Leibniz*, Pittsburgh: University of Pittsburgh Press, 2003, pp. 68–91.

— *Process Metaphysics*, Albany, NY: State University of New York Press, 1996.

— *Process Philosophy: A Survey of Basic Issues*, Pittsburgh: Pittsburgh University Press, 2000.

Ridley, M., *The Origin of Virtue: Human Instincts and the Evolution of Cooperation*, London and New York: Penguin, 1996.

Rorty, R., *Philosophy as Cultural Politics: Philosophical Papers*, Vol. 4, Cambridge: Cambridge University Press, 2007.

Russell, B., *A Critical Exposition of the Philosophy of Leibniz* [1900], London: George Allen and Unwin, 1937.

— *Portraits from Memory and Other Essays*, London: George Allen and Unwin, 1956.

— *The Principles of Mathematics* [1903], London: George Allen and Unwin, 1937.

Ryle, G., 'Fifty Years of Philosophy and Philosophers', *Philosophy* 51, 1976, pp. 381–9.

Schilpp, P. A. (ed.), *The Philosophy of Alfred North Whitehead*, La Salle, IL: Open Court, 1941.

Seager, W., 'Consciousness, Information, and Panpsychism', *Journal of Consciousness Studies* 2, 1995, pp. 272–88.

— 'The Intrinsic Nature Argument for Panpsychism', in A. Freeman (ed.), *Consciousness and its Place in Nature*, Exeter: Imprint Academic, 2006, pp. 129–45.

— *Theories of Consciousness*, London and New York: Routledge, 1999.

Searle, J., *Mind: A Brief Introduction*, Oxford: Oxford University Press, 2004.

Sherburne, D. W., *A Key to Whitehead's 'Process and Reality'*, Chicago: University of Chicago Press, 1996.

Shields, G. W. (ed.), *Process and Analysis: Whitehead, Hartshorne and the Analytic Tradition*, Albany, NY: State University of New York Press, 2003.

Simons, P., 'Metaphysical Systematics: a Lesson from Whitehead', *Erkenntnis* 48, 1998, pp. 377–93.

— 'The Seeds of Experience', in A. Freeman (ed.), *Consciousness and its Place in Nature*, Exeter: Imprint Academic, 2006, pp. 146–50.

Skrbina, D., *Panpsychism in the West*, Cambridge, MA: MIT Press, 2005.

Skrbina, D. (ed.), *Mind that Abides: Panpsychism in the New Millennium*, Amsterdam and Philadelphia: John Benjamins, 2009.

Sprigge, T. L. S., *The God of Metaphysics: Being a Study of the Metaphysics and Religious Doctrines of Spinoza, Hegel, Kierkegaard, T. H. Green, Bernard Bosanquet, Josiah Royce, A. N. Whitehead, Charles Hartshorne, and Concluding with a Defence of Pantheistic Idealism*, Oxford: Clarendon Press, 2006.

— *The Importance of Subjectivity: Selected Essays in Metaphysics and Ethics*, ed. L. B. McHenry, Oxford and New York: Clarendon Press, 2011.

— *James and Bradley: American Truth and British Reality*, Chicago: Open Court, 1993.

— *The Vindication of Absolute Idealism*, Edinburgh: Edinburgh University Press, 1983.

Strawson, G., 'Realistic Monism: Why Physicalism Entails Panpsychism', in A. Freeman (ed.), *Consciousness and its Place in Nature*, Exeter: Imprint Academic, 2006, pp. 3–31.

— 'The Self and the Sesmet', *Journal of Consciousness Studies* 6/4, 1999, pp. 99–135.

— *Selves: An Essay in Revisionary Metaphysics*, Oxford and New York: Oxford University Press, 2009.

Strawson, P. F., *Individuals: An Essay in Descriptive Metaphysics*, London and New York: Routledge, 1995.

Urmson, J. O., *Philosophical Analysis. Its Development between the Two World Wars*, Oxford: Clarendon Press, 1956.

Ward, J., *Realm of Ends or Pluralism and Theism*, Cambridge: Cambridge University Press, 1911.

Weber, M., *Handbook of Whiteheadian Process Thought*, 2 vols, Frankfurt: Ontos Verlag, 2008.

— *Whitehead's Pancreativism*, Frankfurt: Ontos Verlag, 2006.

Whipple, J., 'The Structure of Leibnizian Simple Substances', *British Journal for the History of Philosophy* 18/3, 2010, pp. 379–410.

Whitehead, A. N., *Adventures of Ideas* [1933], New York: The Free Press, 1967.

— *The Concept of Nature* [1920], Cambridge: Cambridge University Press, 2000.

— *Essays in Science and Philosophy*, London: Rider, 1948.

— *Modes of Thought* [1938], New York: The Free Press, 1969.
— *Process and Reality: An Essay in Cosmology* [1929], corrected edition by D. R. Griffin and D. W. Sherburne, New York: The Free Press, 1978.
— *Religion in the Making*, Cambridge: Cambridge University Press, 1926.
— *Science and the Modern World* [1925], New York: The Free Press, 1967.

Index

Absolute, the, 75n, 97
abstraction, 10, 13, 21–2
accident, 51, 82, 96–7
actual entity, 26, 63–6, 69, 73, 80, 102, 111, 124
actual occasion, viii, 41, 53, 58, 61–2, 65, 72, 79, 81–2, 84, 88, 91, 94, 96–7, 102, 105–7, 111
analysis, viii, 34, 67
anthropomorphism, 74n, 105
Aristotle, viii, 25, 32, 41, 73, 80, 97, 108, 110, 117
atomism, 5, 68

Bacon, Francis, 9
Basile, Pierfrancesco, 45n, 59n, 98n
Berkeley, George, 11, 38, 66
Bradley, Francis Herbert, 58n, 75
Broad, Charles Dunbar, 130

Brown, Stuart, viin
Bruno, Giordano, 24–5

categories, 7, 19, 40–1, 49, 52, 67, 70, 80, 119
causation, 13–14, 36, 50–8, 124
Cavell, Stanley, 119
Chalmers, David, 16n, 98n
civilisation, 130
Cobb, John B. Junior, viin, 119
combination problem, 85, 98n
Common Sense, 3, 12, 17, 36, 67
concrescence, 62–4, 69–70, 91, 94, 97, 102, 103, 111, 124
consciousness, 7–8, 13–15, 37–8, 53–5, 58n, 61, 85–6, 95
continuity, evolutionary, 8
contradiction, 21, 24–5
creativity, 96–7, 109, 115, 120, 126

criteria (for the evaluation of metaphysical theories), 17, 20–6

De Volder, Burcher, 35, 45n, 52
decision, 64, 105
Della Rocca, Michael, 15n, 98n
Descartes, René, viii, 6, 11, 14, 22–3, 39–42, 43, 52, 84, 88
Dewey, John, 115–27
Di Poppa, Francesca, 15n
dualism, Cartesian, 11, 22, 44, 67, 71, 72, 84
duration, 53, 69

eliminativism, 7
elitism, 113n
emergence, 7, 95, 105–6, 112
Emmett, Dorothy, viin
emotion, 7, 37, 71, 91, 106, 132
enduring things, 4, 12, 19, 42, 79–84, 88, 92
energy, 91
eternal objects, 80–1, 102, 122, 124–5
events, viii–ix, 3, 11–13, 19, 33, 36, 53, 56, 66, 71, 79, 88, 90, 130
evolution, 5–6, 8, 19, 95–6, 101–4, 112n, 125
Ewing, A. C., 112n

feeling, 37, 48, 53–4, 58, 64, 72, 91, 101–3, 105–6, 112, 134
Ford, Marcus Peter, 46n
form, 64–5, 79–81, 90, 102–4, 107–12, 125–6
freedom, 13, 64, 104
future, 37, 61–2, 74n, 92, 95, 97, 109–9, 122

generalisation, 18–19, 43, 79
God, 6, 23, 50, 58n, 79, 88, 92, 97, 101–13, 124–7
Griffin, David Ray, viin, 58n, 119

harmony, 50, 52, 55, 106
Hartshorne, Charles, viin, 113n
Hegel, George Wilhelm Friedrich, 117
heterogeneity problem, 6, 8–10, 15n, 68, 70, 84, 106
Hick, John, 113n
Hocking, William Ernest, 45n
Hume, David, viii, 36, 38, 52, 65, 101, 126
Husserl, Edmund, 54

idealism, 15n, 24, 61, 66, 71, 97, 116, 119, 121, 123
ideals, 104, 109, 124
identity, personal, 88–9
immediacy, presentational, 36–7
immortality, objective, 57

ingression, 102–3
intrinsic nature argument, 8–10, 16
Ishiguro, H., 45n

James, William, 8, 16n, 37–8, 46n, 52–4, 58, 74n, 85–6, 116, 119, 130
Jowett, Benjamin, 31

Kant, Immanuel, 20, 65
Kim, Jaegwon, 16n

Lango, John, 74n
language, 3–5, 17–18, 71–3, 81, 87, 119
laws, natural, 13, 92–5, 103, 124
Leclerc, Ivor, viin
literature (and philosophy), 4–5
Locke, John, viii, 6, 38, 43, 47–8

McGinn, Colin, 12
McHenry, Leemon, 45n
McTaggart, John Ellis, 130
Mander, William, viin
Masham, Damaris Cudworth, 6
materialism, 5–8, 10–14, 18, 22, 26, 45n, 61, 92
Mates, Benson, 45n
mathematics, 18, 43, 120, 122, 126, 129
Maxwell, James Clerk, 129
memory, 58n, 107

mentalism, 10–11, 66, 71
misplaced concreteness, fallacy of, 10–11
monads, 10, 23, 33–6, 38, 43, 45n, 47–58, 62, 70, 86, 88
monism, 23, 34–6, 68
Moore, George Edward, 24, 129
Moravcsik, J., 97n
Mugnai, Massimo, 45n

Nagel, Thomas, 14, 15n, 98n
nature, bifurcation of, 11, 44, 68, 80
Newton, Isaac, viii, 13, 66, 67, 92, 105
novelty, 102–5, 109, 111, 126

Occam's razor, 23
ontological principle, 26, 102
order, ix, 15n, 62–3, 67, 74, 82, 92–5, 102–5, 116–18, 121, 125–7
organism, 5–6, 42–3, 82–7, 95–6

panexperientialism, 71, 74–5n
panpsychism, 15n, 16n, 71, 74n, 75n, 98n, 105
Parkinson, G. H. R., 45n
Passmore, John, 99n
Peirce, Charles Sanders, 16n, 19, 20, 27n, 98n, 119, 126, 130

perception, 9, 36–8, 48, 50, 53–7, 58n, 65, 70, 82, 86
Phemister, Pauline, 16n
Plato, viii, 15, 31–2, 41, 74, 80, 97n, 103–4, 106, 108, 117, 121, 125–7, 129, 131
pluralism, 33–4
pragmatism, 98n, 130
prehension, 52–8, 62–5, 66, 67, 73, 87, 106, 107
psyche, 74n
psychology, 37, 43, 46n

qualia, 14
quantum physics, 12, 20
Quine, Willard van Orman, 27, 28n

relationalism, 13
relations, 5, 32–45, 50, 52, 55–6, 58n, 61, 62, 67, 68, 86, 92, 98
relativity, theory of, 12–13, 20
religion, 20, 124
religious experience, 20, 57, 101–2
Rescher, Nicholas, 44n, 45n
retention, 54–7, 61
reversion, category of, 102–3
revisionary metaphysics, 3–5, 81

Ridley, Matt, 112n
Rorty, Richard, 119
Russell, Bertrand, 16n, 33–5, 45n, 112, 130
Ryle, Gilbert, viin

Santayana, George, 130
satisfaction, 64, 109, 111
scepticism, 40–2
Seager, William, 16n, 98n
Searle, John, 16n
self, 40–1, 52–6, 58n, 64–5, 72, 84, 88–92
Simons, Peter, viin, 16n
Skrbina, David, 16n, 98n
society, 81–5, 88, 90, 95–6, 101–4, 116, 123, 126
soul, 42, 45n, 46n, 53, 58n, 81–3, 88, 95
space-time, 12–13, 66–71, 80
Spinoza, Baruch, viii, 6, 15n, 22–5, 33–5, 38–9, 67–8, 97, 98n
Sprigge, Timothy L. S., viin, 58n, 59n, 75n, 113n
Strawson, Galen, 14, 15n, 46n, 58n
Strawson, Peter Frederick, 3, 15n
subject-predicate form of thought, 4, 34, 49, 67
subjective aim, 64

subjectivist principle, 52
substance, viii, 6, 11, 13, 22, 23, 31–44, 47–9, 51–2, 64, 67–8, 71, 73–4, 80–2, 88–9, 92, 97, 106, 108, 123
substantivalism, 13
sufficient reason, principle of, 7, 15n, 25–6

universals, 80–1, 107
Urmson, O., viin

vacuous actualities, 5, 9, 93

Ward, James, 98n, 130
West, Cornell, 119
Whipple, J., 15n

EU representative:
Easy Access System Europe
Mustamäe tee 50, 10621 Tallinn, Estonia
Gpsr.requests@easproject.com

www.ingramcontent.com/pod-product-compliance
Lightning Source LLC
Chambersburg PA
CBHW051118230426
43667CB00014B/2641